The Losantavilles vs. The Crescents - 1888
Cincinnati, Ohio

~New Ideas for~
CRAFTING
HERITAGE
ALBUMS
WITHDRAWN

BEV KIRSCHNER BRAUN

...ternal S...
...ther, Albert Joseph Mumm...
...his brother, Joseph P., is on his ri...
...ther, John, brother of Albert, is the 1st in the back ro...
This may have been a championship baseball game because they
appear to be wearing ribbons on their uniforms,

R.S.
1716/E

Baptismal   Cer

BETTER
WAY
BOOKS

CINCINNATI, OH

ABOUT THE AUTHOR

Bev Kirschner Braun lives near Cincinnati, Ohio with her husband, Dave, and two dogs. Bev is a project manager for a national health insurance company. She is the author of *Crafting Your Own Heritage Album* and teaches classes on heritage albums and genealogy part-time.

New Ideas For Crafting Heritage Albums. Copyright © 2001 by Bev Braun. Manufactured in China. All rights reserved. No part of this book may be reproduced in any form or by any electronic or mechanical means including information storage and retrieval systems without permission in writing from the publisher, except by a reviewer, who may quote brief passages in a review. Published by Betterway Books, an imprint of F&W Publications, Inc., 1507 Dana Avenue, Cincinnati, Ohio 45207. (800) 289-0963. First edition.

Other fine Betterway Books are available from your local bookstore, art supply store or direct from the publisher.

05 04 03 02 01   5 4 3 2 1

Library of Congress Cataloging-in-Publication Data

Braun, Bev.
    New ideas for crafting heritage albums / by Bev Kirschner Braun.
        p. cm.
    Includes bibliographical references and index.
    ISBN 1-55870-580-5 (alk. paper)
    1. Photograph albums. 2. Photographs--Conservation and restoration. 3. Scrapbooks. I. Title
TR465 .B73 2001
745.593--dc21   2001025013

Editor: Jane Friedman
Photography: Christine Polomsky and Al Parrish
Designer: Joanna Detz
Production artist: Kathy Bergstrom
Production coordinator: Kristen Heller

ACKNOWLEDGMENTS

A special thank you to family and friends who made contributions to my personal heritage collection with photographs, memorabilia and documents. You've given me terrific items for layout pages in my personal heritage album and to use as examples in this book.

Special acknowledgments go to Jan Dufour, Pam Boedeker and Patsy Bunch for contributions of their heritage pages as examples here also.

To my mother, Maxine Millennor Kirschner, thank you for saving all the family treasures for me for so many years and thank you for being the best mother and friend any daughter could ask for.

To my in-laws, Mary and Bill Braun, thank you for sharing your photographs and for having such a wonderful son to share my life with.

DEDICATION

To Dave

INTRODUCTION ❧

When I first began creating scrapbook pages, I experimented with traditional color cardstock and old photographs. After the first few pages, I knew this is what I wanted to spend my time doing—creating a heritage album for each of my family lines. Now, only a few years later, I have hundreds of completed layout pages documenting my heritage.

I take my heritage albums to family reunions and holiday get-togethers. Everyone thoroughly enjoys looking through the pages and reading the journaled details. Family members are fascinated by the large extended family we've identified over several generations. Sharing the family history makes our reunions more meaningful and more fun, and gives everyone a true sense of family. As we look around at the several generations of family members in attendance, we see the similarities in their looks and mannerisms with the photographs and stories we have of our ancestors.

My heritage collection has grown by leaps and bounds over the past few years. It's difficult to keep everything organized. I've found new cousins from different branches of the family that I didn't know about before. Some I've found through the Internet and some through family and friends. We share information and keep each other motivated to look for just one more piece to the puzzle.

Many people want to know how the Internet can help them with their genealogical research. With the changes in technology, you can get things done faster and, in most cases, cheaper than ever before. Genealogical research is a very enjoyable and rewarding hobby, and for some a lucrative and worthwhile profession. If you haven't started your research yet, I encourage you to get started as soon as you can. You'll meet many wonderful people who are also searching for their heritage. You become part of a large community with the same objective rather than being out there on your own pursuing something no one else has any interest in.

Heritage scrapbook makers are the same. When you get together in a group to work on your albums, the time just flies by. There is never enough time to finish all the things you want to do once you actually find the time to sit down and start working on your pages. You get inspiration from one another by looking at the creativity that goes into showing off your family treasures.

My inspiration for creating *New Ideas for Crafting Heritage Albums* is to give you encouragement, ideas and guidance on some of the current techniques and technological tools available to help you discover and share your ancestral heritage with family and friends. My hope is that the creative motivation you may need to produce a unique, well-documented family heritage album will come from information in this book. You may want to do more in-depth research and learn more about some of the technology tools and techniques on your own. The heritage album seeds have been planted. It's now up to you to nurture them and help them grow into a treasured family heirloom.

CHAPTER 1
Scrapbook Basics

The first step in creating your heritage album is to gather your photographs, memorabilia and documents. Look everywhere for things to put in your album. Look in old photo albums, closets, dresser drawers, the attic, the basement and the garage. Look at pictures and anything else that might already be framed. Talk to your family, especially the older members; they may have bits and pieces of information that will help you on your way.

GATHERING AND ORGANIZING

Gathering all of your family history collection in one location is a good start. As you begin to organize your collection, you'll probably be surprised with just how much information you have to work with. Ask family and friends of your family if they have items they can share with you. Once you get the first few pages of your heritage album completed and share them with family members, they may be much more willing to add to your collection.

ORGANIZATION

Organization is so important when creating a heritage album, as it is in any other project you work on. Most of us have our family treasures spread all over the house. The more time you spend organizing and planning up front, the more time you'll be able to spend actually working on your album.

Find a clean work area to use while you are organizing your collection. You will need a large table where you can spread things out, sort them into stacks, and begin putting items into the appropriate storage containers until you get ready to put them into your heritage album.

INFORMATION TO SAVE

There are so many items you can save and include in your heritage album. Keep these items organized so you can easily find them when you want to add them to your heritage album. Collect anything that will give meaning and purpose to your heritage album. These articles will help explain what was going on in a person's life at a specific time in history.

Everyone has an old suitcase or junk drawer with heritage items in it.
Gather them and create a priceless family heirloom with a heritage album.

Information to Save

- newspaper articles about family members or close friends

- diplomas, certificates of achievement, special awards

- invitations, announcements (birth, engagement, wedding, graduation)

- family tree information

- death information (obituary, memorial and prayer cards)

- military records

- college or high school transcripts, old report cards

Awards and special achievements should be included as part of your heritage album. Future generations can only appreciate the significance of these awards if they know about them.

Documenting family relationships will help current and future family members easily recognize their family lines.

What to Include

You will have many items as you sort through your collection. To ensure a well-documented history of each person or family in your heritage album, here are suggestions on some items to include:

- information about primary person's spouse and family members (parents, siblings, children)
- pictures of primary family members with names and relationships to you
- graphical representation of immediate family members, such as an ancestral or pedigree chart
- copies of official documents (birth, death, baptismal, marriage, naturalization papers, land deeds) that will prove your heritage
- time lines of major known facts about the family (employment histories, residences, births, deaths, marriages)
- information about family members' occupations, where they attended school, the homes they lived in over the years
- personal histories about family provided by oral histories, family members, family traditions, anecdotes, historical documents, published family history stories
- personal family mementos to share with future generations (war medals and military dog tags, hospital birth bracelets, picture lockets, hobby samples, old cigarette cases)

ARCHIVAL INFORMATION

To ensure your heritage album won't start deteriorating in twenty to thirty years, you must use 100 percent archival products. Archival means materials are acid-free and chemically stable to ensure acids won't eat away your photographs and documents. You are creating a priceless heirloom for future generations and do not want to worry about its longevity after all your hard work.

As well as the items that will actually go into your heritage album, you need to preserve the rest of your collection for future generations. There is other information on proper preservation of photographs, documents and memorabilia in this book. Be sure to read the information to help you determine just how to store your items so they will not suffer damage and deterioration.

This is an example of acid migration caused from the newspaper that was adhered directly to these pages in the early 1930s.

LAYOUT BASICS

Look through scrapbook and craft magazines to see some of the ideas that others have used to design their pages. Also check out the resource section in the back of this book for scrapbook web sites. Most of these have heritage album sections you can get ideas from.

Do not clutter your pages, and always leave plenty of room for journaling. Remember, you are documenting your family history. You need to tell the story that goes along with the pictures and documents on your pages.

Estelle Schaeper and Faye Kispert

Estelle is the daughter of John Schaeper and Cecelia Finke.

Her mother was the sister of Mary Amelia Finke Mummert, mother of Edna Mummert Murphy and Helen Mummert Efkeman.

Estelle and Mary Efkeman Braun are cousins.

This simple design creates a classic heritage page layout that includes the details and relationship information.

MULTIPLE PAGE LAYOUTS

Sometimes your heritage layout will require more than one page. Make sure the information is presented side by side so the viewer knows what goes together. Using coordinating papers also helps tie the pages together.

However, don't make all of your layouts multiple pages just because you have a lot of photographs. Choose only the best ones, and give the rest away or put them in a photo album to include in one of your other scrapbooks.

Either of these pages could stand alone in your album. By placing them side by side, they really make for an elegant two-page layout.

FOCAL POINT

Ask yourself, "When people look at this page, what do I want to be sure they see and read? What is the story behind the pictures? What memories do I have that I can share with others to make this page more interesting?" Each page should have a focal point.

Decide what photo or document you want to stand out on the page, and then arrange other items around it.

Choose one to two photographs to focus on your message; use a bolder, larger font (either hand-written or computer) to draw atten-

tion; choose color and paper weight that work best to deliver your message; or place the photograph at an angle to focus attention on it.

By setting the photograph at an angle, you draw the viewers to focus on that first then to the other items on the page.

Creating a Focal Point

- Use different types of fonts—headings larger than subheadings.

- Contrast bold vs. semibold vs. plain.

- Put bolder colors behind important information areas to make them stand out.

- Leave white areas around information.

- Pick best location—reader usually starts in the upper left corner.

- Place pictures at a slight angle.

- Put picture next to important journaling since it will attract the eye and reinforce the focus.

- Put a shape or border around the type, or give it an interesting shape.

- Use reverse type (white lettering on black background) to draw attention to it.

BALANCE

Good balance means that each side of the page has the same visual "weight." Decide if your page can be divided into equal halves, quarters or thirds. Each section of your page should be a mirror image of the other section or sections. Each item you add on your page adds weight—mats on your photos, journaling and embellishments all add different degrees of weight to the page. The secret is to keep these weights balanced so that no one section of the page looks too heavy.

This two-page layout is pleasing to look at because both pages appear to be visually equal even though the photographs are different sizes on the two pages.

BORDERS

When you are designing a page layout, consider using a simple border, which can enhance the color on a page. Many borders are fast and easy to do. They take up only a little space on the page, leaving lots of room for photographs and journaling.

The type of border you use will determine how much space you have remaining on the page for the rest of the layout. Use plain or decorative paper, fancy scissors, paper punches, fancy rulers and pens, stickers, and clip art. There are many examples of fast and simple borders on the layouts in this book that you can copy or adapt for your own pages.

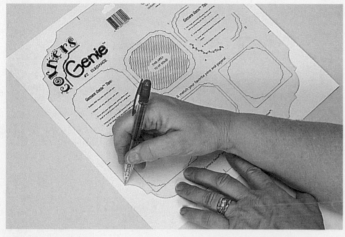

Using the Corners Genie template, trace the design on the wrong side of the paper with a light pencil.

Use a craft knife to cut out the design. Use the middle piece on another coordinating layout.

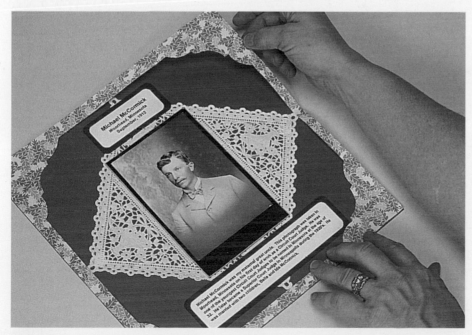

Place the outside border on your layout page. Adhere the border to the page with permanent acid-free adhesive when the design is complete.

PAGE TOPPERS

Simple page toppers can illustrate the focus of your layout. You can buy them ready-made, make your own using your computer and color printer, or use alphabet templates. Whichever method you choose, page toppers can add to the overall themes on your album pages.

Family members attending the 50th Wedding Anniversary Party of Warren and Duane Millennor on July 26, 1998.

Above: Nancy and Don Millennor
Right: Siblings--Ethel, Barb, Warren, Don, Max
Below: Alice, Sue, Max, Bev
Bottom Right: Warren and Duane with grandchildren—
Front: M'Elise, Kaitlan, Ryon
Back: Duane, Michelle, Warren, Melanie, Steven, Melissa, Kara

Page toppers create a focal point and enhance your heritage pages.

Warren Delphus & Duane Allen Millennor
Married April 3, 1948 in Cincinnati, Ohio

50th Wedding Anniversary Party
Blue Ash, Ohio July 25, 1998
Above with their children:
Mike, Jim, Pete, Donna and Sue

JOURNALING

Journaling is what makes a heritage album different from a photo album or scrapbook. Always try to include as much information as you can for your family now and in the future. This may be information people won't remember unless it is documented.

Our memories are too elusive to be depended upon. Stories are passed down from generation to generation, but they may lose some of the details and accuracy depending on who is listening and who is retelling the stories. If you want to keep the facts straight (or if you want to pass along a family legend that may have questionable details to it), write down the story and include it.

Your heritage album is a work in progress. If you don't know what the story behind the picture is right now, leave enough space on the page to add information later. As family and friends look through your book, they may be able to tell you a story or give you additional information that you will want to include with the pictures.

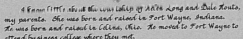

A know little about the courtship of Adèh Long and Dale Houts, my parents. She was born and raised in Fort Wayne, Indiana. He was born and raised in Celina, Ohio. He moved to Fort Wayne to attend business college where they met.

Mother told me she sat in the same desk Daddy did one class period apart. Notes were left like the one on the next page and a romance was begun.

It was a story of city girl meets county boy. Mother was not at home on the farm. When she would visit the Houts farm, she dreaded walking the path to the outhouse. There was a mean old gander which actually chased her up the slanted roof on one of the buildings

Mother also told me she and Daddy drove to Celina to tell Grandma and Grandpa Houts that they had gotten married. As the visit was winding down, Mother went to the car so Daddy would have time alone with his parents to share the news. Daddy came out, got in the car and was driving down the road when Mother inquired as to how Grandma and Grandpa had taken the news. Daddy had lost his nerve and did not tell them. At Mothers insistence, they turned around and drove back to the farm so Daddy could tell Grandma and Grandpa he was a married man.

I love this story because it is so unlike Daddys in charge, corporate decision maker self.

Documenting details about your ancestors is a valuable part of your heritage album—even if there are no pictures to go with the stories.

JOURNALING EVERYDAY EVENTS

It is important to capture everyday events in our lives to let others know what a routine day is like. These are the memories that we lose over time because we tend to forget the routine days and remember only those when something significant happened.

How many times have you wondered what your parents or grandparents did on a typical Saturday? Capture your typical memories, and document them for your children and grandchildren. Keep items from everyday lives that may be significant pieces of the past for future generations.

This letter was written by my mother, Maxine Millennor Kirschner, to her family after moving to a country farmhouse 25 miles from Cincinnati, Ohio.

Country Farmhouse Memories

This photograph was taken on the same day as this letter was written. This shows all six kids in the barnyard of our new country farm. My oldest sister Alice (7) holding the youngest brother, Steve (13 months), third oldest brother Randy (4), oldest brother Barry (8 1/2), and second oldest brother, Dan (5). That's me (Bev-age 3) holding my head wondering just what Mom and Dad were thinking when they moved us so far from the city and civilization.

This letter is one of my favorites. It tells what a typical week was like for our family in 1955. The letter actually survived for over 18 years. My grandmother took it with her when she moved to California in the mid-1960's. Her daughter, Alice Joy, returned it to my mother after the death of their mother, Anna Maria Droll Millennor, in August 1973.

This letter explains what a typical week was like for my family in 1955. This letter is a wonderful example of a real treasure for a family historian.

TELLING THE WHOLE STORY

When you are including photographs on your pages, always include names, ages, dates, places and events, if you know them. If you don't know what the story is behind the picture, ask relatives or friends who might know more about the photograph.

When you begin to think about what to write, try to answer questions that someone might have when they are looking at what is on the page. Questions such as:

- Who is in the photograph (names, ages)?
- Where was the picture taken?
- When was it taken, and who took it?
- What were they doing?
- Who are they related to?
- Why do they look so happy or sad?
- What other details can you tell about in the photograph, such as a car or house?

Documented information and accurate details add valuable information for viewers of your heritage album.

INCLUDING GENEALOGICAL INFORMATION

The journaling in your heritage album should always include basic genealogical facts. Include names, birth and death dates, relationships to you and other family members ("parent of" and/or "child of," etc.). Include as much information as you have on events in family members' lives, such as when and where they were born, when and where they were married, what they did for a living, what property they owned, and who their neighbors and friends were. This information will help family and friends piece together the family relationships.

Remember that you are documenting your family history and this information is critical to the overall validity of your heritage album. It doesn't matter if the information is handwritten or displayed in a chart form as long as it is documented and accurate.

If you are including genealogy documents, include the source information. You must do your research and validate the information. Others will know you have validated the data if your sources are listed along with your documentation.

If the document is a court record, include

- name of the court (indicate if it is a local, state, or federal court)
- name of the building where it was found
- what city or town it is in
- volume, page number, document record number, and date found

If it is a church record, list the name and address of the church.

It is important to include information about the sources of your documents in case someone needs to obtain another copy to validate their research.

Using Scraps for Journaling

When using a computer for journaling, you can waste a lot of good paper trying to get your journaling to fit exactly where it should on the page. Try this easy technique to use your scrap pieces of cardstock paper to journal on your pages.

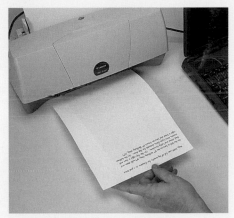

Type your journaling into your computer and set your margins to fit the space you want.

Print on plain white paper first to see if it fits the space on your layout page.

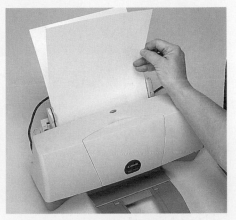

With temporary adhesive, secure a piece of scrap cardstock over the printed journaling on the white paper.

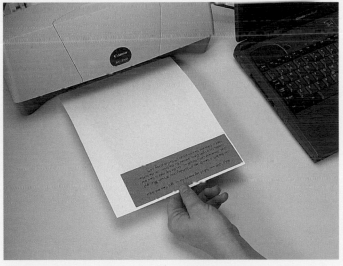

Feed back through the printer so it prints on the scrap paper this time.

Remove the scrap paper. Put permanent adhesive on the back, and adhere to your final layout page.

Grandpa McKern 1897

CHAPTER 2
Photographs and Documents

Preservation of photographs and documents is of utmost importance if they are to last for future generations. Proper care and storage using archival products will help ensure that they will. You must also take the time to document your photographs. If you have a collection of old photos with no information about them, ask family members to help you identify any information they can. Someone may give you valuable information.

PHOTOGRAPHS AND FAMILY HISTORY

Photographs are such an important part of our everyday lives that we sometimes take them for granted. We can purchase a throwaway camera for just a few dollars. We take our pictures, turn the camera in for processing, and end up with great pictures, and we don't have to worry about taking care of a camera or film. We record our memories on film with little effort—reunions, marriages, graduations, births, major events, cemetery visits, etc. With the aid of technology, these memories can be shared with family and friends around the world in a matter of minutes.

Photography is a great way to help preserve family history and heritage. When we include photographs with our family history findings, we make our heritage much more interesting and alive to those who read it. Photographs help us pass on a part of our histories that cannot be captured any other way. Photos illustrate and document people, places and things

that cannot be adequately conveyed through words alone. So take the time to preserve your heritage by properly caring for your photographs for future generations.

DOCUMENT YOUR PHOTOS

You need to treat photographs in the same manner you would any other item you collect as part of your family history. It is just as important to document your photographs as it is the other genealogy documents you acquire. There is specific information that should be included in your documentation.

• Give the full name of each person in the photograph (and if it is a group picture, each subject's position in the picture).

• Document exactly where the photograph was taken, including the city, county, state, county and full date or at least an approximate time period.

• Document any specific information such as the event (wedding, birth, family reunion), or if it is at someone's house, at a historical location, etc.

• If you know who took the picture, list that also. If you took the picture, note any information you can think of that will help preserve the memory of the photograph.

• If you send a lot of digital photographs, some software will allow you to include text. Give as much of the above information as possible so the photograph retains its history.

Use a photographic marker to document details on the back of each photograph. These special markers will not damage or bleed through to the front like a ballpoint pen or pencil will. These pens are inexpensive and are available at photography and craft stores or by mail order from scrapbook and photography suppliers.

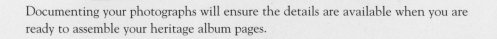

Documenting your photographs will ensure the details are available when you are ready to assemble your heritage album pages.

Taking Better Photos

Picture too dark

Wrong shutter speed or film speed may have been used; check camera settings. Electronic flash was not properly recharged; there may not have been enough light for a simple camera. You might have been too far away from your subject for the flash to give you enough light.

Picture too light

You might have been too close to the subject and the flash created too much light; check the manual for your camera and flash to see what the proper distances are. You may have used the wrong film speed, or the shutter speed was too slow.

No picture

Camera shutter did not open. You may have left the lens cap on when taking pictures. You may have accidentally taken an unexposed roll of film in to have it processed. In 35mm cameras, the film may have failed to advance.

Blurred picture

There might have been camera movement. Shutter speed on a 35mm might be too slow; use a higher shutter speed. Maybe you were too close to the subject, or focusing may not have been set at the proper distance. If just the person in the photo is blurred, he or she may have moved when you took the picture.

Light streaks or fogging

Check to make sure the camera back is closed tightly after loading the film. Load your film into the camera only in the shade or low light of an indoor room. Don't open the camera back until you are sure the film is rewound into the canister.

Correcting white eyes in pets requires a special pet correction pen. There is also a red-eye pen for people.

THE ENEMIES

There are three enemies in the life of your photographs: humidity, light and temperature. Exposing your photographs to any of these will speed up the deterioration process.

HUMIDITY

If at all possible, photographs should be stored in a room in your home that maintains a relative humidity (the amount of moisture in the air) between 30 and 40 percent. If the climate you live in goes up and down a lot, store photographs in an air-conditioned room. Use a humidifier (to add moisture) or a de-humidifier (to reduce moisture) to help safely store your photographs and documents.

LIGHT

It is a natural process for a photograph to begin fading as soon as it is printed and light hits it. How long the fading process takes depends on how your photographs are stored. Store photographs in acid-free storage boxes and photo sleeves until you are ready to put them in your album. Use only archival products in your heritage album to ensure photos won't be damaged. Do not display photos under bright indoor lights or in direct sunlight.

TEMPERATURE

Photographs are covered with a light-sensitive coating made up of silver and gelatin called an emulsion. If you've ever left a photograph in your car on a hot summer day, you've seen it warp and curl as the emulsion became soft and shifted. Photographs should not be exposed to temperatures above 75°F. If your photographs are accidentally exposed to a higher temperature for a short period of time, put them in a room that is between 60 and 70°F and let them cool to room temperature before handling them.

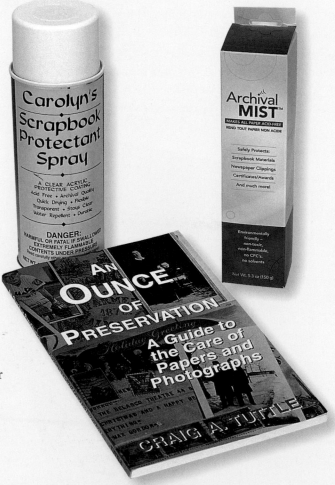

To learn more about caring for your photographs and documents, do your research and use only archival-safe products in your heritage album.

PHOTO PRESERVATION

COLOR PHOTOGRAPHS

All color photographs will eventually lose their color. It can take anywhere from 20 to 60 years depending on several factors. If you have color photographs that are 20 or 30 years old and are beginning to fade, have them reprinted if you have the negatives.

Some professional photography shops will use archival-quality paper if requested. This can be expensive and it takes more time, so you will want to be selective about which photographs you request to have printed this way. Most commercial labs use the same type of chemicals and techniques, but some use different types of paper to print your photographs. Do a little research to see what papers are best, and select a commercial lab that uses the better papers.

Improper care and storage have caused these photographs to deteriorate over time.

HANDLING

Your hands should be clean and oil free when handling photographs and documents. Oil and dirt can rub off your fingers and onto the documents and photos causing damage and deterioration. Using a pair of inexpensive photography cotton gloves will help keep oily fingerprints from causing long-term damage.

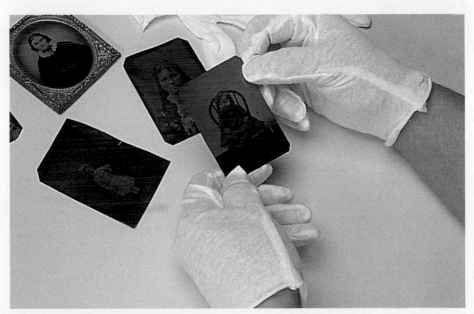

When handling photographs and documents, protect your heritage collection by wearing photographic cotton gloves.

Paper Preservation

Documents, newsprint, color photographs and books printed on poor-quality paper are all prone to deterioration due to the acid in the paper. The poorest quality of paper is usually newsprint and tends to be the first to deteriorate. It will turn brown and brittle. Another problem that causes paper deterioration is acid migration. This occurs when low-quality paper bleeds onto neighboring pieces of paper. Some old letters, invitations, or documents may have brown stains on them that were caused by the acid migration. The better the quality of the paper, the less acid migration you will see.

For some paper items, the best solution is to photocopy the information on acid-free buffered paper. This works especially well for newspaper clippings. Place the photocopy in your heritage album. Store the original document in an acid-free page protector to help preserve it because it may continue to deteriorate.

You may want to include the original document in your heritage album. For those items, use Preservation Technologies Archival Mist de-acidification spray. It allows you to remove most of the acid content from paper and newsprint. You spray both sides of the document or newspaper item with Archival Mist, and this product will help protect paper against deterioration and crumbling for hundreds of years. You can then place the treated newsprint or document in your heritage album on a mat of buffered paper to reduce further acid migration. Archival Mist cannot be used on photographs.

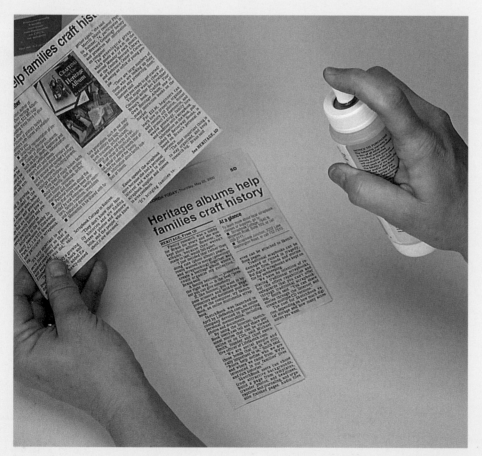

Safe and easy-to-use Archival Mist neutralizes acids in paper and coats it with an alkaline buffer to protect against future exposure.

MOUNTING PHOTOGRAPHS

ORIGINAL PHOTOGRAPHS

Decide first if you are going to include original photographs in your heritage album. I suggest you make duplicates of these and store the originals in a safe place. However, if you decide you do want the originals in your album, there are some great choices for mounting that will allow you to remove the photos at a later time if you need to make copies.

PHOTO CORNERS

Photo corners are easy to apply and hold your photographs securely, although you can remove them from the page, if necessary. Photo corners come in black, gold, white, transparent and a variety of pastel colors. Some are self-adhesive and others need to be moistened to activate the adhesive on them. I found it is easiest to put the photo corners on each corner of the photograph and then attach the corners to the mat or album page.

Acid-free photo corners provide an attractive way to mount your photos without permanently adhering them to the page.

CORNER SLOT PUNCHES

Decorative corner slot punches are punches that add a beautiful decorative enhancement to the photo mat without taking away from the photos. You can easily slip the photographs off the mat and replace them again since no additional adhesive is used on the page.

Decorative photo corner punches are another option for placing photos if you want to remove them later.

PHOTOCOPYING PHOTOGRAPHS

An inexpensive option I use most is to make photocopies of photographs on acid-free paper. This is an economical way to make good-quality copies of just the photos you want to use in your heritage album. You can make beautiful copies of black-and-white photos on a color copy machine by setting it on the black-and-white setting. Put the copy in your heritage album, and store the original photograph using one of the safe storage methods mentioned in a later section.

PH-Neutral Pen

Be sure the paper in the photocopier is acid-free. Carry your pH-neutral pen with you, and check the paper before you spend money making your copies. Remember:

Blue (line doesn't change colors)—no acid

Green (line changes from blue to green)—some acidity in the paper

Yellow (line changes from blue to yellow)—too much acid in the paper to be safe

This example shows the photocopy of the original photo made on regular paper and then on photographic paper. Either copy is good enough to be included in your album. The original can then be stored in a safe place.

These color photocopies look as good as the original photos for use in your heritage album.

PHOTOCOPYING DOCUMENTS

Sometimes important documents (or photocopies) are not in very good condition. You can clean them up and make copies for your heritage album so they look more attractive without taking away from the authenticity.

If you have photocopies of documents, try copying them onto a cream-colored paper to make them look older and more authentic.

Another reason to photocopy documents for your heritage album is so that you can resize them to fit on the page with the rest of your layout.

Photocopying documents allows for resizing to fit your layout page.

This original document (on the left) is too large and too fragile to include in your album. A reduced photocopy (on the right) offers a better option for your album page.

KODAK PICTURE MAKER

Another great option is to use the Kodak Picture Maker systems available in many of the national chain stores to make copies and enlargements of photos without negatives. You can make duplicate photographs in different sizes from wallet size to 8" x 10". Other features can enhance pictures as they are being made. Using this system, you can intensify the photo's color if it has faded, zoom in and crop out unwanted background items, eliminate red-eye, and add borders, words, and other options. If you are new to using this system, ask the store associate for help. The store usually has at least one person who has been trained and really knows how to use all the features on these systems. He or she can show you some cool stuff to make your photos look great.

Four individual photographs were scanned and printed on one page using the Kodak Picture Maker systems.

Storage

What should you do with all the photographs and negatives you now have? Sort through them and decide which photos to keep for your heritage album and which photos to give away or file.

Store those you decide to keep in archival safe negative protector sleeves, and keep them in three-ring binders. This will protect your photographs from rubbing against each other and from being torn or crushed. Archival-safe sheet protectors will hold larger photographs and protect them from oily fingerprints, dirt, dust and spills.

Sort the photographs and keep them in acid-free shoebox-type photo boxes. If you are not sure they are acid-free, line the inside with acid-free buffered paper. Change the buffered paper periodically to ensure any acid migration from the box to the paper does not harm your photographs. If you make your own dividers for your photo boxes, also use acid-free buffered cardstock for these.

To prevent damage or further deterioration to the old letters, documents, photographs, and newspaper clippings in your collection, store them safely until they are placed in your heritage album.

Proper storage is important to preserving your family documents and photographs. It can significantly increase the life span of any piece of paper . Light, humidity, heat and improper handling of paper cause the most reduction in a paper's life span.

Warning!

Do not store your negatives and photographs together. I suggest keeping the negatives in a bank safety-deposit box or at someone else's house. If a disaster strikes, like a fire, flood, or tornado, and your photographs are destroyed, you will still have the negatives if they are stored in a separate place.

Here's another storage option: Record details of special events on the outside of the acid-free Easy Sort Envelope System and enclose your photos, documents, negatives and memorabilia on the inside.

Paper Storage Tips

• Place a document or newspaper clipping between two pieces of blank archival-safe paper, which can then be thrown away if acid migration occurs.

• Place paper items in archival-safe page protectors to prevent them from rubbing against each other and causing further deterioration. Store papers open and flat, not folded.

• Don't hang one-of-a-kind documents or photographs in direct sunlight. They will quickly fade and deteriorate.

• Don't use self-adhesive tapes or glue to repair torn paper or book-binding. In the long run, it will cause more damage to the paper. There are several types of acid-free adhesive tapes that can be used on the backs of photographs to repair them.

• Don't laminate family heir-looms and one-of-a kind documents unless you use a copy of the original. This will not prolong the life of the paper and cannot be undone.

• Don't use staples, paper clips, or other metal objects with paper, as they will eventually rust.

• Don't store documents or photographs in attics (usually hot and humid) or in basements (usually damp). They should be stored in a cool, dry place.

Acid-free paper and photographic storage units will protect your documents and photographs from damage and deterioration.

PHOTOGRAPH RESTORATION

If you have a one-of-a-kind photograph to be repaired or restored, don't attempt to make any physical repairs yourself. Take the photograph to a qualified professional photographic conservator. This process is expensive, sometimes ranging from $50 to as much as $250, but the results will be worth it if it is done correctly. Expensive restorations should be displayed in archival-safe frames out of direct sunlight. If you decide to have restoration work done, do your research so you understand exactly what is involved.

HOME SCANNING

A less expensive option is to use a home flatbed scanner, scanning software and a photo-quality printer attached to your computer. A flatbed scanner is a piece of equipment that connects to your personal computer.

Photo-imaging software is fairly simple to use, and most scanning software offers several features to allow easy restoration of old photographs. Do some research and check with friends and family to see what they use and what they like best. You can get great results with photographs and documents using these features if you learn how to use a scanner and the software correctly. Read the user's manual (or help section online that comes with the software), and practice doing photo restorations on your computer. You must have a good photo-quality printer to get the best results when printing your own photographs.

Photo-imaging software features allow easy restoration for your heritage album photos.

ARCHIVAL PRINTER INKS AND PAPER

Until recently, ink cartridges in most photo-quality printers have not been considered archival and permanent. Photographs printed were expected to last only about three to four years. If you store your photos digitally, you can always reprint them if they begin to fade. Now, there are several new photo-quality inkjet printers being offered with both archival and permanent ink available. More will be offered in the future, so check to see which models offer archival and permanent inks before investing in a new inkjet printer.

New inkjet printers offer standard archival and permanent ink cartridges. When used with heavyweight matte photographic paper, they produce a beautiful image that should last twenty years or more. If you are in the market for a new photo-quality printer, be sure to do your research and find out which printers and inks are best for the type of work you will want to do. If you are printing all of your own images for your heritage album, take precautions to ensure images won't fade five years from now. There are also archival sprays for your printed photographs to protect and help them last longer.

Great restoration results using home scanning software and your computer can bring old photos back to life.

The restore option in the photo-imaging software allowed for quick repair of the tear in this original photograph.

RESIZING DIGITAL PHOTOGRAPHS

Sometimes your photographs and documents are just too small or too large to fit the layout you have designed. If you have the items in a digital format (such as scanned, on CD-ROM, or on a diskette), you can print them on a photo-quality printer in just about any size you need.

Digital formats of your photos allow you to enlarge them to fit the design you've chosen for your layout page.

These photographs were scanned and resized so they would both fit on the layout page.

CREATING NEGATIVES

If you have an old photograph but no negative, you can have a copy negative made.

A copy negative is made of an original photograph and then additional photographs can be made from the new negative. During the duplication process, corrections can be made to the new negative to improve the quality of the finished photograph. You can also request archival-quality finishing and paper from the photographic lab to add to the long-term stability of the copy negative and print. A copy negative allows you to produce reprints in quantities and provides you with protection for your precious family photographs so they won't deteriorate and be lost forever. Remember to store the new negative in an acid-free negative sleeve and keep it in a safe storage place.

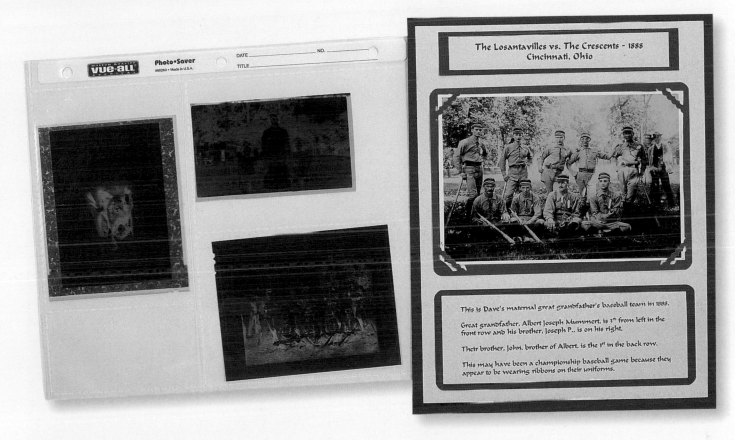

This photograph was originally taken in 1888, but the negative was lost over time. A copy negative was made from the photograph, and additional photos were then made from the new negative.

PHOTOGRAPHIC PAPER SCRAPS

Save those scrap pieces of photograph paper and put them to good use. Here are a few quick steps to help you use those scraps to print great photographs for your heritage album. Your photos need to be in digital format to begin this process.

1. Print a copy of the photo onto plain paper to see what position it will be on the paper.

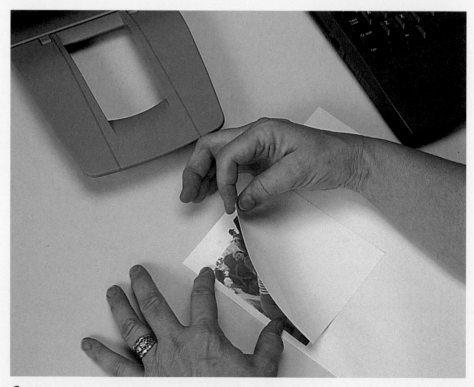

2. Select a piece of scrap photographic paper slightly larger than the finished photo size.

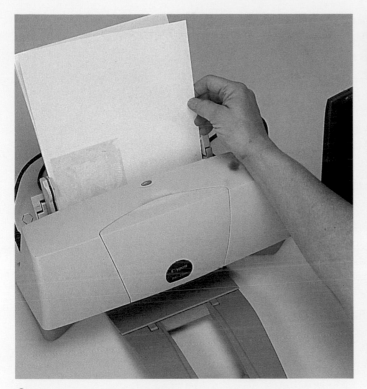

3. Place temporary adhesive on the back of the photo paper, and place it over the original print on the white paper.

4. Feed the white paper back through the printer and reprint the photograph in "best" mode so it prints on the photo paper this time.

5. Remove the printed photograph from the paper. You may need to crop or mat it before using it on your layout page.

GOING DIGITAL

Everyone wants to know, "What's the big deal about digital cameras and how do I know if I need one?" The answer may just depend upon what you want to use the camera for. Take a look at the advantages and disadvantages listed below; once you've decided that you do indeed want a digital camera, there are a few specific features you need to look for (besides just the price).

DIGITAL CAMERAS

Make sure the camera you are thinking about purchasing is compatible with your home computer. Not all of the software is compatible with both the Macintosh and PC-compatible computers.

Consider the resolution or pixels. You want to consider a minimum of two megapixels (resolution in the thousands). The higher the pixels, the better the resolution you will get and the larger the photograph you can print without it looking distorted. Remember, the higher the pixels, the faster your storage medium will fill up.

Another item to consider is the storage capacity. This determines how many photographs you can store before you need to download the images to your computer. Low-end digital cameras may not have any storage capacity, which means you have to download your images right away to a diskette or your computer. The minimum you should consider is 8MB but a 16MB will allow you to take approximately twenty to thirty digital photos before you have to download them. You should also consider a camera that allows you to review the photos you have taken and delete any you don't want, which frees space to take more photos.

Consider a camera that allows you to take closer shots of people far away or take close-up shots of documents, cemetery headstones, landmark signs, etc.

Whatever camera you decide to buy, make sure you read the owner's manual carefully. You will want to be able to use the camera to its fullest capabilities. Practice using the camera before you go to an important event or have the opportunity to take that once-in-a-lifetime shot. You don't want to miss it because you don't know how to operate the zoom or don't know how to tell how much storage space you have left on the memory module.

PROCESSED FILM STORAGE

If you currently have a 35mm camera, whether it is a single lens reflex (SLR), a disposable, or something in-between, you don't have to rush out to buy a new digital camera to take advantage of the newest technologies. Several film processing options will give you some of the same benefits as a digital camera. You still have to take or send the film to be processed, which means the photos won't be available instantly. But with the following options, you won't have to figure out how to sort and store all those extra photos or the negatives you don't want.

Digital Photography

Advantages

- Instant—there's no waiting in line for processing.
- You know immediately if the photo is in focus and you have the shot you want. If not, you may have the opportunity to retake it.
- The same memory card records images and transfers them to your PC or other digital storage device—no more film.
- Print only those images that you want.
- Delete images from your memory card and keep only the ones you want as you are taking photographs, which reduces the number of bad photos you end up with.
- You don't have to sort and store extra photos and negatives.
- You can share digital photos with family and friends instantly using e-mail or a web page.

Disadvantages

- Equipment (camera, computer, printer, photo paper, ink) is expensive.
- Only a few inkjet printers offer archival and permanent ink. Images will only last three to four years if you do not use the newest printers with archival and permanent inks.
- Images can be displayed only on computer screen, or you need a photo-quality printer that accepts the memory card directly so you can print onto photo paper.
- You have to keep images organized and file names meaningful to be able to find an image if you need to print it.
- Images can occupy an enormous amount of your computer's hard drive, so you need to know which file type to save them in or save them to disk.

DISKETTE

Having your film transferred to a diskette is the most economical way to digitize your photographs. It costs around five dollars for twenty-four to twenty-seven photos. Most stores also include the software that you need to retrieve the images on the diskette. The downside of this is that the photographs are saved at a low-resolution, which means that if you want to print a photo larger than a 3" x 5" it will look distorted. You have to be careful with the way you store the diskettes because they are prone to damage.

CD STORAGE

This option costs about twelve dollars at the time of processing—about one-hundred images on CD. This would allow you to take pictures of your heritage album pages and store them on a CD as a backup. There are different types of CD storage, so when shopping for this option, check to see which is better for your needs—CD-ROM (read-only) or a CD-RW (erasable/rewritable) drive.

Photographic images stored on CD are expected to last fifty to one-hundred years or more, if they are properly cared for according to published specification by the manufacturers. This means storing them in a safe environment (dust free and stable humidity) and handling them only by the edges.

Storing your images on your hard drive of your computer is not the best method of storage. If something

There are many options available if you want to store your photographs in digital format rather than having processed prints and negatives.

happens to your hard drive, you've lost all of your images. You need to keep a current backup copy of them every time you add more images. If you keep them on CDs, you will be able to use them on any computer that has a compatible CD or DVD drive (CD-ROM, CD-RW or DVD-ROM drive).

When you copy your images to a CD it also automatically changes the file to a read-only file so that you don't accidentally write over that image. You can do this on your hard drive, but it is a manual process for each file that you save as an image.

ONLINE PROCESSING SERVICES

There are several online services where you can save your images online. (See the resources section for details.) Each offers some special

features, so check them out before you decide which one to use. You may want to use different services for different processing depending on the purposes of the photos.

TRANSFERRING TO DIGITAL

You can also have any of your photographs, negatives, documents and artwork transferred to a digital format at any time. It is best to have it done at the time of the processing, but if you have any of these items that you would like transferred to diskette, online or to a CD, you can have that done. Check with your local photo-developing centers to see what services they provide.

CHAPTER 3
Memorabilia

As you gather your heritage collection, you will find all kinds of memorabilia to include in your album. One way or another, you can display just about anything you have. Included in this section are just a few examples and options for displaying some of the bulkier three-dimensional items. New products for showcasing memorabilia are coming out on the market everyday to help preserve and protect your family treasures.

ALBUM DISPLAY

You can display just about anything in a heritage album. Some items might be too heavy or would be damaged if they were put in your heritage album and handled a lot. You could take a color picture or make a color photocopy of the item to include on the album page. Many options are now available for displaying items such as small booklets, jewelry, award ribbons and medals, ticket stubs, coins, etc., right in your heritage album.

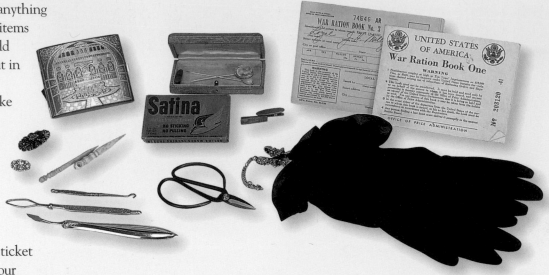

Here are just a few of life's little treasures that you can include in your heritage album.

OVERSIZED ITEMS

Sometimes your memorabilia may just be too large to include in your heritage album. Here are a couple of suggestions to include copies of an item so the memories and the story can be passed on to future generations. You can make color photocopies of the memorabilia and include it on the page along with your journaling.

You can also take a photograph of family members with their memorabilia and include it on the page with the journaling.

This family heirloom is almost one-hundred years old and is too large to include in a heritage album. Make a photocopy of the tablecloth and include it along with the photograph and documented information. The original can be stored in an acid-free box and tissue paper.

Photograph or photocopy memorabilia such as a graduation cap and gown, place it on the page with journaling, and don't forget to show the graduate.

Acid-free vellum pages can hold items you may want to remove and read. Print directly on vellum envelopes with your inkjet or laser printer.

MEMORABILIA POCKETS

These are clear, archival-safe, self-adhesive pockets in a variety of sizes for encapsulating items that may contain acid, but that you want to display in your album. These would hold small, almost flat items, such as coins, a lock of hair, sand from your beach vacation, ticket stubs, note cards and cassette tapes. The pockets have full adhesive backs that are ready to stick on your paper. They have self-adhesive flaps that you can close and open as often as you like.

Family Portrait
John and Kathrine Roggentien of Williamsburg, Iowa
With daughters Lucy, Pearl, and Molly

Katherine always made all clothes for the family. Notice the bows for each of the girls that were made to match their dresses. The cameo pin above is the same one Kathrine is wearing on her dress in this photograph taken around 1903.

(Above) This cameo pin can be removed to wear and easily returned to this memorabilia pocket.

(Left) This cigarette case from the 1930s will become a family heirloom over the next few generations.

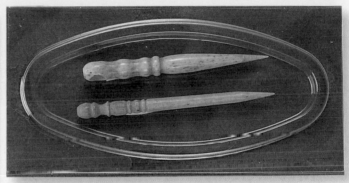

Memorabilia pockets come in a variety of sizes to hold small 3D items on your pages.

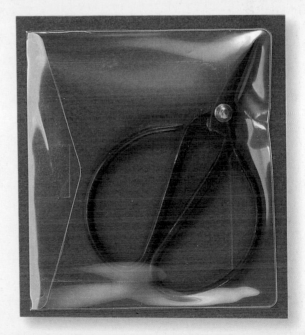

These eyeglasses worn in the photograph are a perfect example of memorabilia you should include with your photographs and journaling in your heritage album.

Sallie Mae Bollander

Sallie Mae and her husband, Thomas, ran the General Store in Ripley, Ohio from 1878-1927. Their store was located on Red Oak Creek right on the northern edge of town. Their home was located out back of the store. They were known to open the store at any hour of the day and night whenever someone needed supplies. Sally Mae was a very small, petite woman, but no man or woman every tried to take advantage of her. She was said to have a heart of gold unless you crossed her. Then it was almost impossible to get back into her good graces. After selling the store in 1927, Sallie became the local piano teacher until her death in 1953 at the age of 95.

TREASURE BOX

Some items are too large to fit into a heritage album, but you'll want to preserve them. Decorate an acid-free Highsmith Keepsake Case so you can share the items with future generations.

KEEPSAKE KEEPERS

Display three-dimensional items in acid-free archival safe plastic trays. They come in two sizes, 8½" x 11" and 11" x 14", that include four to six different-shaped compartments totally enclosed and fully visible. They are hole-punched to fit into most scrapbooks.

The acid-free Keepsake Keeper will hold your three-dimensional memorabilia and fit in your heritage album. Items can be removed and replaced back in the Keepsake Keeper for storage.

The larger Keepsake Keeper is also three-hole punched to fit in your album for attractive display and easy archival storage.

CLEAR POCKET HOLDERS

Some of the memorabilia you have will be best displayed by using a simple clear pocket holder on the page. Make these yourself by cutting down a clear page protector to the exact size you need. Use a clear permanent adhesive to close the edges and adhere it to the page. Leave the top or one side open to insert the booklet or card. Make a photocopy of the inside of the item to display on the page so viewers can see what is inside the booklet or card without taking it out of its holder.

A clear pocket page allows you to remove and replace this booklet on this page.

Generations Memorabilia Envelope will encapsulate items such as this mortarboard in a three-hole-punched, archival-safe envelope right in your heritage album.

Generations Slash Pockets are ideal for including these kids' journals made in elementary school about their family history.

3D KEEPERS

These antique hooks for buttons and boots can easily be included on your album page using archival-safe 3D Keepers.

3D Keepers come in a variety of sizes and shapes to display your memorabilia in your heritage album.

VIDEO AND AUDIO CARE

Preserving family memories on video-cassette recording (VCR) tapes has been very popular over the past decade or so. However, VCR tape is even more fragile than color photographs and you need to take extra precautions to ensure proper storage and handling of these tapes.

VCR tapes, like photos, are subject to harmful reactions from light, humidity and heat. These elements can cause chemical reactions that speed up the tape's deterioration. Dirt is also a deadly enemy of the VCR tape. Usually, dirt gets into the VCR and scratches the tape, causing a loss of the image over time.

VCR tapes are expected to last about ten years. If proper care and storage precautions are taken, it is very possible that another high-quality copy of the VCR tape can be made to preserve your memories.

Videotapes should be stored in an archival box on end in an air-conditioned room to help preserve them longer.

Tips on Audio and Video Preservation

• Make a backup copy of your original tape that you will keep in a safe place. This copy can later be used to make another copy when the original begins to deteriorate. Also, break off the tab on a video-cassette to prevent accidentally re-recording over the original tape.

• Minimize tape handling at all times. Avoid dropping them.

• Buy only high-quality VCR tapes. There are reports that are published in magazines and on the Internet that will let you know what brand-name tapes are best for

what you want to record. Cheap VCR tapes are not going to last nor be good enough to preserve your family memories.

• Store VCR tapes and cassettes standing vertically upright, on their ends. Audio or videocassettes should not be stored lying flat.

• VCR and audio tapes should not be stored in the rewound or fast-forwarded position. You should play a tape completely through, then store it without rewinding. Wait to rewind it just before playing it again.

• Keep an eye on changing technology. You may need to have your audio and videocassette tapes copied to a newer medium in the future. Fifty years from now, there may not be any playback devices available to play your audio and videocassette tapes. So keep up with the technology changes and have your precious memories transferred to a new medium to ensure you will be able to still play and see those memories in the future.

PRESERVING CLOTHES

Now that the big day is over and you have all the pictures you need of the big event, it's time to think about how you want to preserve your christening or wedding dress.

The christening dress shown here is over 150 years old. It has been used for four generations of christenings and multiple times during each generation. To ensure that it will last another 150 years, it must be properly cleaned and stored.

You first need to have the dress professionally cleaned by a company who specializes in cleaning and storing of christening, Communion and wedding gowns. Don't take the dress to just any local dry cleaner. Make sure the cleaner knows how to properly clean and care for your gown. I wouldn't trust it to someone who has to send it out to have it cleaned. Have it cleaned on the premises, and make sure you are able to look it over carefully when you pick it up. Some cleaning services will seal it in a storage bag before you pick it up. If this happens, you'll have no way to know that it was cleaned and is in good condition before you store it.

After it is cleaned and you have inspected it, it is ready to be stored in archival-safe materials. You will need to get acid-free and lignin-free tissue paper and a storage box big enough to comfortably store the dress without cramming it in. The gown should be wrapped in tissue paper before it is folded in the box. The tissue paper will protect the fabric from rubbing against itself and from creating permanent folds in the dress. Do not store the dress hanging on a hanger. The weight of the fabric will weaken the fibers and stretch the dress out of shape.

Place it in an acid-free box after wrapping it in the tissue paper. Store it lying flat, and don't place anything heavy on top of it. The ideal storage area is in an air-conditioned room where the temperature stays fairly constant year round and is low in humidity—similar to the same storage conditions for your photographs and documents.

The general guideline costs for having a wedding gown professionally cleaned and for a preservation package to store it in will cost about $200 to $350. A christening dress cleaning and preservation package will run around $60 to $125. These costs will not include the cost for any restoration processes (if the dress has turned yellow or the fabric needs to be repaired).

You may need to change the tissue paper and box about every two to three years to ensure no damage occurs to the fabric of the dress as a result of acid buildup. You can use your pH-testing pen from your scrapbook supplies to test the tissue paper and box to be sure no acid has built up on either.

If you cannot store the dress in an air-conditioned part of your house, there are other types of packing boxes that museums use that will help protect it more from heat and humidity changes. These are harder to find, but you can check with professional conservator services and on the Internet to find sources for these boxes.

Whenever you handle the dress, it is a good idea to wear a pair of cotton gloves. This will keep any dirt or oil from your fingertips from getting on the fabric.

Proper storage of fabric heirlooms helps ensure they will be around to be worn by future generations even after one-hundred years—as this christening dress has been.

WALL DISPLAY

Another option for sharing your family heritage items is to display some of your old photographs. If you decide to do this, you need to take some precautions to ensure your photos are displayed safely and will not end up with damage or deterioration.

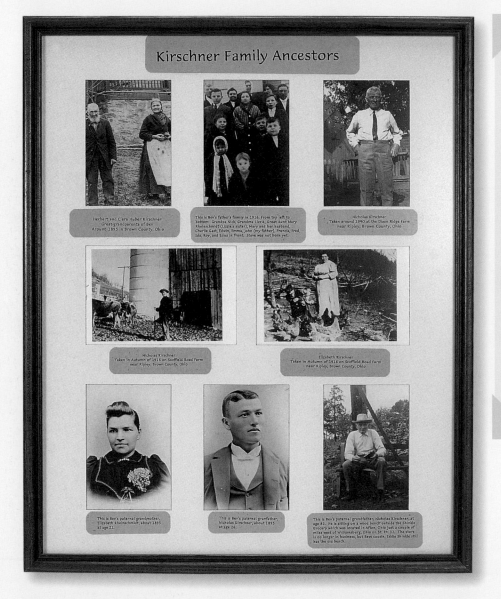

These are photocopies of photographs displayed in an inexpensive photo collage frame. Details were added under each photograph to identify these ancestors for family and friends.

Rules for Display

• Don't hang photographs in direct sunlight or under bright indoor lights. It is best to be able to control the amount of light that hits the photos.

• Use ultraviolet filtering Plexiglas and archival, acid-free paper in the frame behind the photo if you are displaying originals.

• Keep a close eye on the originals to ensure they are not fading or deteriorating in any way.

• Make copies of your original photographs and display the duplicate copy instead of the original.

• Keep food and beverages away from your display area. Accidental spills can cause irreversible damage.

Share a family marriage record by displaying it in a frame. Keep it out of direct light, and use an archival-quality frame to protect it from fading and deterioration.

This confirmation document is too large to include the original in your heritage album. Make a photocopy for your album, and display the original in an archival frame.

Oatmeal Refrigerator Cookies

Ingredients:
½ cup soft shortening
½ cup sugar
½ cup brown sugar—packed tight
1 egg
½ teaspoon grated lemon rind
½ tablespoon molasses
1½ teaspoon vanilla
½ cup sifted flour (equals 7/8 cups)
7/8 cup sifted flour
½ teaspoon soda
½ teaspoon salt
1½ cup rolled oats

Mix in bowl: shortening, white and brown sugar,
1 egg, lemon rind, molasses, vanilla.
Stir vigorously 'till smoothly blended.

Sift into bowl:
sifted flour, soda and salt
Stir gently till smooth.

Add rolled oats, stir. Make
into ball of dough. Pat on waxed paper.
Roll 5 inches × 2½ in. diameter.
Chill dough in refrigerator 'till ready to cook.
Remove, use thin sharp knife, slice thin
(1/8 inch) Place on lightly greased sheet - 400°
from 8 to 10 minutes

PANS

to 2 deep 9" pie pans
preheated to
350° -
to 50 minutes or
heat down
clean in center

CHAPTER 4

Family Recipes

Recording your family's food-related traditions is just one more way to preserve your ancestral history. Family recipes and food play an intricate part in the job of recalling our lifelong memories. Adding photographs and stories with these recipes ensure the memories and traditions can be carried on by present family members and future generations.

CAPTURING MEMORIES

Over the years, the kitchen has always been the main gathering place in our home, in my parents' home, and in my grandparents' home. All kinds of memories come to mind when I remember the family meetings, the birthday parties, Sunday afternoon dinners, the wedding and bridal showers, and sports events. It seems all of those memories include food—a great appetizer, a full-course meal, or just some scrumptious dessert that was to die for. Not only does the food conjure up memories, but the sounds of laughter, conversation, music and dishes clanging add to those memories.

When we built our house, we skipped the formal dining room. We knew our family and friends would be more comfortable in a big old-fashioned open kitchen with the dining area at the far end. This way everyone could congregate in the kitchen before, during and after the meal. And they do. We also opted for two large porches—one on the front and one on the back of the house. With such a large family, the only sit-down dinners we have are buffet-style meals. You fill your plate then grab a chair wherever you can find one and strike up a conversation with whomever is nearest. That's about as formal as it gets at our house.

These are the memories you want to capture for your heritage album. Memories are not just about great recipes that have been enjoyed for as long as you can remember, but all the other remembrances as well. We want to know who tells the best (and worst) stories during the family gatherings and which family members always get the party going when they show up. Record some of the funniest memories your family has about past food disasters. Like the burnt brownies Uncle Mike thought he'd cover up with icing and Grandma Jane's annual holiday fruitcake sent out every year that has been buried in the bottom of the freezer for the past several years.

And don't forget to keep the camera handy if you are going to start capturing these traditions for future generations. Sometimes a picture can be worth a thousand words, but it is always better when we add our journaling to the page with all the details of what was going on in the photograph.

Remembrances of family gatherings and good food are special memories we want to capture for all times.

Family recipes passed down from generation to generation are heirlooms that are commonly overlooked when we are researching our family histories. Family recipes can reveal specific details about our ancestors that may be difficult to uncover in other ways. They can reveal what region of a country our ancestors came from and the religion they embraced. Gathering these recipes and taking the time to prepare them for family and friends to enjoy is one way to celebrate your ancestry.

Just about everyone has special memories associated with food. Even though the food created from our special recipes may be delicious, what really makes them special for us are the memories associated with that favorite dish or dessert. These are the memories that we especially want to capture. Some of those memories come from our childhood, and some from friends and family during our adult lives. They need to be written down and kept as part of our family histories so they are not forgotten.

People may ask, "Why was it so special to you?" Now you can let them and future generations know just what was so special about the food and the memories you keep telling them about. By writing down these memories along with the recipe, and adding a photograph or two, you can keep these memories alive. Family members are much more likely to try these recipes and create their own special memories if they can appreciate the meaning behind why one is so special to you.

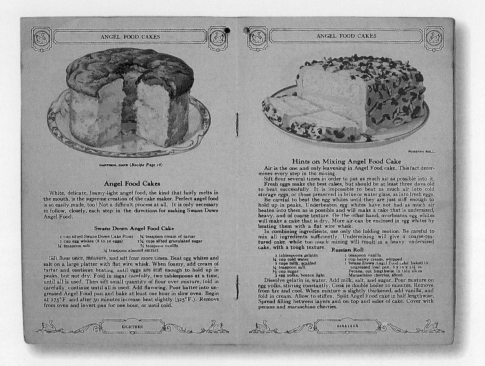

You can almost smell the delicious cakes baking in the oven as you look over the recipes in this old family cookbook.

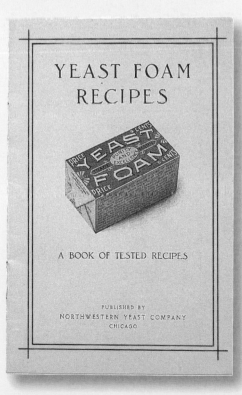

Old family cookbooks can add important details related to your ancestor's culinary pleasures plus add important historical facts to your family history.

AWARD WINNING RECIPES

We may have special recipes from past generations that are considered just so special we wouldn't think of not including them in our albums. Some of them are award winning, and some of them should be. In our modern world of fast food and microwaves, there is little time to cook and bake. Some of the best recipes may never be shared with our families and friends unless we take the time to document the recipes and our memories. After all, some of the memories we have can only be appreciated with pictures and the words that go with them.

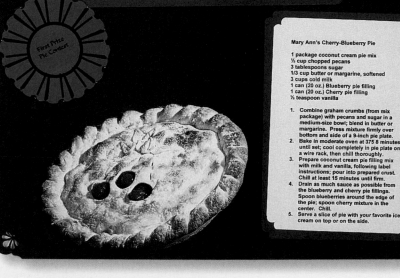

The original recipe for this award-winning pie was lost many ears ago, according to my Aunt Mae. Her mother made this pie from "scratch" (which means nothing came out of a can or a box). Aunt Mae was able to recreate the recipe and everyone agrees it is as good as the original.

Aunt Mae was nine years old when her mother entered this pie into the pie-baking contest at the Clarke County Fair on the 4th of July in Ohio. Her mother walked away with first prize 4 years in a row. She adds, "the only reason Mother didn't win a fifth year was because a strong windstorm knocked over the prized cherry tree. She had to use cherries from a neighbor's tree that just weren't the same. They had a whole different texture and taste".

Aunt Mae said she baked this pie every year for the annual family picnics because it reminded her so much of her childhood. She said she never entered the pie in a contest. She'd just be too disappointed if she didn't win. Now others in the family take turns baking the same pie each year so the recipe and memories stay with us.

Aunt Mae

First Prize
Pie Contest

Mary Ann's Cherry-Blueberry Pie

1 package coconut cream pie mix
½ cup chopped pecans
3 tablespoons sugar
1/3 cup butter or margarine, softened
3 cups cold milk
1 can (20 oz.) Blueberry pie filling
1 can (20 oz.) Cherry pie filling
½ teaspoon vanilla

1. Combine graham crumbs (from mix package) with pecans and sugar in a medium-size bowl; blend in butter or margarine. Press mixture firmly over bottom and side of a 9-inch pie plate.
2. Bake in moderate oven at 375 8 minutes until set; cool completely in pie plate on a wire rack, then chill thoroughly.
3. Prepare coconut cream pie filling mix with milk and vanilla, following label instructions; pour into prepared crust. Chill at least 15 minutes until firm.
4. Drain as much sauce as possible from the blueberry and cherry pie fillings. Spoon blueberries around the edge of the pie; spoon cherry mixture in the center. Chill.
5. Serve a slice of pie with your favorite ice cream on top or on the side.

Special memories like these are certainly priceless additions in your heritage album.

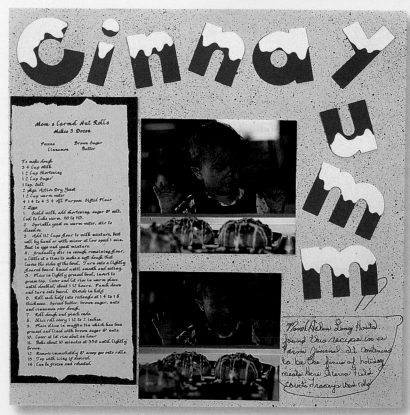

HOLIDAY MEMORIES

Many of our most special memories are traditions we've carried out during our many holidays such as Hanukkah, Christmas, Kwanzaa, Easter, July Fourth (Independence Day in the United States), Thanksgiving Day, Valentine's Day and Mother's Day (or Mothering Day as England refers to it).

If you want these traditions to last, it is a good idea to record your memories associated with specific holidays. Some of these traditions have been carried on for so many years, we may not even remember the true beginning of these holidays and traditions.

Many countries celebrate holidays in a similar manner but with slightly different traditions. If your family celebrates these holidays, you may want to do a little research and find out how your family traditions differ from those of your ancestors in their home country.

An example is that both Canada and the United States celebrate Thanksgiving Day. However, these holidays are celebrated at different times of the year and have very different traditions associated with them. These traditions and memories need to be captured so future generations can see the differences, especially if your family includes members from both countries and you want to celebrate both the United States and Canadian Thanksgiving holidays.

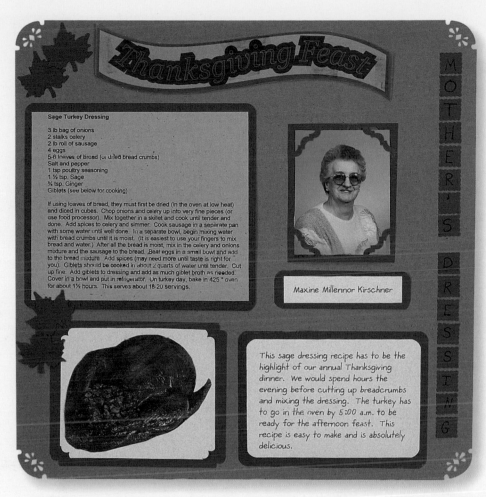

This sage dressing recipe has to be the highlight of our annual Thanksgiving dinner. We would spend hours the evening before cutting up breadcrumbs and mixing the dressing. The turkey has to go in the oven by 5:00 a.m. to be ready for the afternoon feast. This recipe is easy to make and is absolutely delicious.

Maxine Millennor Kirschner

Renowned family recipes handed down for generations should be the first ones we document and include at our annual family holiday gatherings.

THANKSGIVING

In the United States, Thanksgiving Day is the number one food holiday. More food is consumed on Thanksgiving Day than on any other day of the year. (The second food holiday is Super Bowl Sunday—the annual ultimate American football game celebration.) Thanksgiving Day in the United States is always celebrated on the fourth Thursday of November. The traditional turkey dinner (stuffing, cranberries, yams, and pumpkin pie) is something few of us will forget if you have experienced it. Thanksgiving Day in the United States commemorates the first harvest feast with the Pilgrims and the Native American people.

THANKSGIVING IN CANADA

The Canadian traditional Thanksgiving meal is very similar to that in the United States. The Canadian harvest comes earlier in the fall, so Canada celebrates it on the first Monday of October and it has nothing to do with the Pilgrims.

CHRISTMAS

Christmas is celebrated in the United States and in England with pretty much the same traditions.

In England, Christmas is a particularly special time. The preparations begin several weeks in advance as both the traditional Christmas cake and Christmas pudding need to be made at least a month before to allow their flavors to develop. In both the United States and England, homes are decorated with garlands, a Christmas tree, and often holly wreaths. Children place stockings above the fireplace in the hope that Santa Claus will leave them a present on Christmas morning. In England, sometimes children leave out a mince pie on Christmas Eve to thank Santa for their presents (and a carrot for Rudolph the red-nosed reindeer). In the U.S. cookies and milk are the traditional treats for Santa. In both countries, gifts are opened on Christmas morning before breakfast.

Everyone has special recipes and recollections to share during the holidays that have become a tradition over the years.

NEW IDEAS FOR CRAFTING HERITAGE ALBUMS

Traditions are sometimes just annual family gatherings that we can take for granted if we don't capture the memories. Let others know just why these get-togethers are special.

The '84 reunion was held at Aunt Wilma's and Uncle Cal's which was formerly Grandma's and Grandpa's homestead.
Opposite Page
Top: John, Pam, Annie, Cal and Mark
Center: Brownie (Arden), Gary and Patti backs of Ruth, Ruth Ida and Lucille
Lower Left: Tesa husband, Don, and daughter, Tara with Pam and Annie
Lower right: John and back of Lyle
This Page
Left: Don Kable and Wilma
Center: Brenda and fiance, Dave
Bottom: Gary's daughter, Trina, with Chris and Annie

CAKES

BIRTHDAY CAKES

Around the world, it seems that birthdays are always a special time for children. A birthday is sometimes the highlight of the year. Family and friends send birthday cards and buy presents. The home is often decorated with balloons or streamers, and there is usually a special birthday cake with candles to celebrate each year of the person's life. People have parties to celebrate with family and friends; this usually consists of a special meal, which ends with the birthday cake and everyone singing "Happy Birthday." Not everyone may have wonderful memories associated with his or her birthdays. However, just a simple card or saying, "Happy Birthday" to someone can make her feel a little special on her day.

Take the time to record these memories, and if you baked a cake, include the recipe and a photograph even if the cake wasn't "baked from scratch ingredients."

Birthday cakes have been a tradition for generations in our family—enjoyed by young and old alike.

Family traditions can start with any generation. Start one with your family and make sure you capture the details so the traditions and memories are carried on.

SPECIAL OCCASION CAKES

We commemorate all kinds of special occasions with a cake as the central part of sharing our joy and best wishes for all who take part in these celebrations. We observe special achievements in our lives, such as graduations, baptisms, job promotions, anniversaries, retirement parties, and weddings. Cakes are an easy way to help celebrate these special days.

Many families have at least someone in the family who enjoys making and decorating the cakes for all of these celebrations. Or, you can always go to the local bakery or supermarket and have a cake decorated with whatever theme you want for your next festivity. Don't forget the camera, and be sure to include the details of these special memories on your heritage album pages.

Wedding memories are some of the happiest memories we have. Weddings are often large, lavish affairs or can be simple, private celebrations. Most people have special memories of weddings throughout their lives—whether their own or someone else's. Wedding guests always check out the wedding cake to see what is special about it compared to others they have seen. There is usually a lot of food, whether the family made it themselves and brought it to share with the guests or had it catered in grand style.

Many special occasions are celebrated with cakes. Be sure to include these happy memories in your heritage album.

EVERYDAY TRADITIONS

Not all food memories are associated with holidays, birthdays or other special occasions. Some of our memories may be associated with everyday events in our lives that happen throughout the year. These just may be the best memories of all that we can capture and pass along to our descendents.

If you can't think of any traditions that you celebrate throughout the year, think about starting one or two. A friend was telling me that every September family and friends celebrate the harvest moon with a big bonfire and campout at a campsite on a nearby lake. They have been holding this annual party for almost seventy-five years now. Whatever weekend the harvest moon falls on

that year, that is the weekend of their fall festivities and campout.

I asked her how it got started and she told me that when her parents were children, they lived on neighboring farms. When the harvest moon came out, it was so bright that it meant a couple more hours of light that they could finish harvesting the crops from the field. After the chores were finished, families and neighbors would sit around a campfire at the edge of this lake and share stories about things that had happened to them and their families during the past year. Even though some of them no longer work on farms or are actually harvesting crops, they still carry on the tradition of gathering around the campfire and sharing

stories with family and friends. Over the years, they began to bring covered dishes and desserts, and it has turned into more of a harvest feast that lasts long into the night—therefore the overnight campout also became a part of the tradition for many of them.

Some of our fondest memories are related to the everyday meals and desserts we remember just because the foods are so tasty and special. Every time we think of them or taste them, a flood of memories comes back to us. So make the time to take a few photographs, write down those recipes and the memories that go with them. Your family will be grateful you did.

This recipe has been passed down for generations in my family because it is simple to make and so delicious.

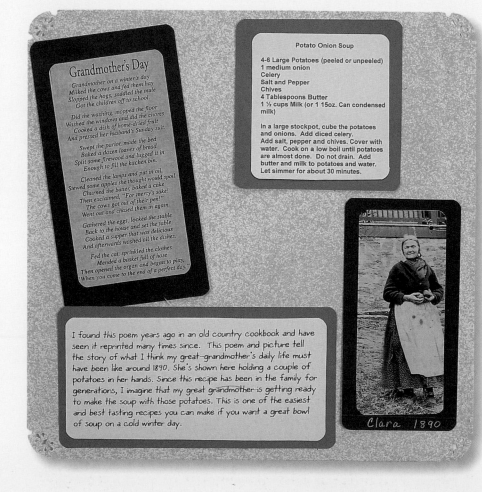

Grandmother's Day

Grandmother on a winter's day
Milked the cows and fed them hay
Slopped the hogs, saddled the mule
Got the children off to school.

Did the washing, mopped the floor
Washed the windows and did the chores
Cooked a dish of home-dried fruit
And pressed her husband's Sunday suit.

Swept the parlor, made the bed
Baked a dozen loaves of bread
Split some firewood and lugged it in
Enough to fill the kitchen bin.

Cleaned the lamps and put in oil,
Stewed some apples she thought would spoil.
Churned the butter, baked a cake
Then exclaimed, "For mercy's sake!
The cows got out of their pen!"
Went out and chased them in again.

Gathered the eggs, locked the stable
Back to the house and set the table
Cooked a supper that was delicious
And afterwards washed all the dishes.

Fed the cat, sprinkled the clothes
Mended a basket full of hose
Then opened the organ and began to play,
When you come to the end of a perfect day.

Potato Onion Soup

4-6 Large Potatoes (peeled or unpeeled)
1 medium onion
Celery
Salt and Pepper
Chives
4 Tablespoons Butter
1 ½ cups Milk (or 1 15oz. Can condensed milk)

In a large stockpot, cube the potatoes and onions. Add diced celery.
Add salt, pepper and chives. Cover with water. Cook on a low boil until potatoes are almost done. Do not drain. Add butter and milk to potatoes and water. Let simmer for about 30 minutes.

I found this poem years ago in an old country cookbook and have seen it reprinted many times since. This poem and picture tell the story of what I think my great-grandmother's daily life must have been like around 1890. She's shown here holding a couple of potatoes in her hands. Since this recipe has been in the family for generations, I imagine that my great grandmother is getting ready to make the soup with those potatoes. This is one of the easiest and best tasting recipes you can make if you want a great bowl of soup on a cold winter day.

Clara 1890

Chocolate Lovers Delight!

This chocolate recipe book has been in our family for generations. My maternal Great Aunt Rachel Harrison is legendary for fixing just about every recipe in this booklet for any special occasion that came along. We were never allowed to have sweet candy when we were children. But, we were always allowed to have at least some of any recipe Aunt Rachel cooked up. We know it was because our mother wanted to eat some of the chocolates and didn't want to seem selfish by not letting us have some also. Whatever the reason, we loved everything Aunt Rachel made. Every once in awhile, one of us will get this book out and try one of the recipes. They are all simply delicious and easy to make!

Great Aunt Rachel Harrison

You can almost smell the chocolate in the room as you read over this recipe!

MORE FOOD FUN

This one-skillet recipe conjures up memories of cold winter nights and a kitchen filled with wonderful aromas.

This page recalls the famous fried chicken recipe shared at many wonderful family outings.

Recipes are even more special when we have them in our ancestor's own handwriting.

Shannon, Patsy, DeShannon and Denise would pack up the car a go back home to Kentucky for the holidays. This meal was at Grandpaw Willie Bunch's house. It was Denise's Birthday and Thanksgiving 1981.

Dinner Rolls.

3 Table spoons lard.
1 — " " sugar.
1 tspoon — yeast.
1 Eggy.
1 Pkg YEAST.
1 cup warm water.
1½ cup flour.

Mix lard, sugar, salt, Eggy to gether. then put yeast in ½ cup warm water then put & mix. then 1 cup flour then ½ warm water ½ cup flour mix to gether. let Rise for 30 min or Double in size. then empty on floured Bald then spoon out in Muffin Pan 3 little Balls let Rise again for about 30 min & Bake.

Mable Faulkner's famous dinner rolls.

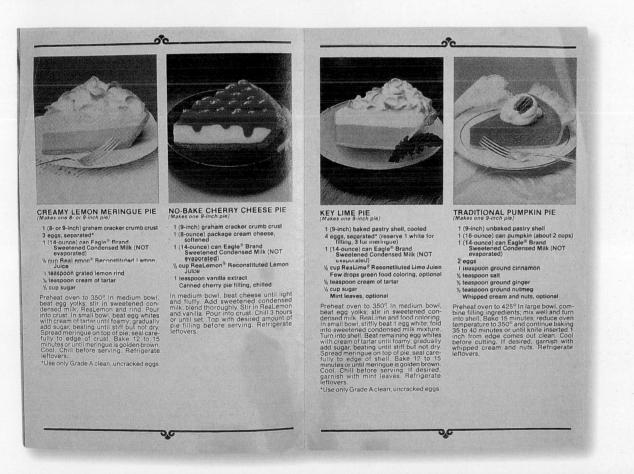

CREAMY LEMON MERINGUE PIE
(Makes one 8- or 9-inch pie)

1 (8- or 9-inch) graham cracker crumb crust
3 eggs, separated*
1 (14-ounce) can Eagle® Brand Sweetened Condensed Milk (NOT evaporated)
½ cup ReaLemon® Reconstituted Lemon Juice
1 teaspoon grated lemon rind
¼ teaspoon cream of tartar
⅓ cup sugar

Preheat oven to 350°. In medium bowl, beat egg yolks; stir in sweetened condensed milk, ReaLemon and rind. Pour into crust. In small bowl, beat egg whites with cream of tartar until foamy; gradually add sugar, beating until stiff but not dry. Spread meringue on top of pie; seal carefully to edge of crust. Bake 12 to 15 minutes or until meringue is golden brown. Cool. Chill before serving. Refrigerate leftovers.

*Use only Grade A clean, uncracked eggs.

NO-BAKE CHERRY CHEESE PIE
(Makes one 9-inch pie)

1 (9-inch) graham cracker crumb crust
1 (8-ounce) package cream cheese, softened
1 (14-ounce) can Eagle® Brand Sweetened Condensed Milk (NOT evaporated)
⅓ cup ReaLemon® Reconstituted Lemon Juice
1 teaspoon vanilla extract
Canned cherry pie filling, chilled

In medium bowl, beat cheese until light and fluffy. Add sweetened condensed milk; blend thoroughly. Stir in ReaLemon and vanilla. Pour into crust. Chill 3 hours or until set. Top with desired amount of pie filling before serving. Refrigerate leftovers.

KEY LIME PIE
(Makes one 9-inch pie)

1 (9-inch) baked pastry shell, cooled
4 eggs, separated* (reserve 1 white for filling, 3 for meringue)
1 (14-ounce) can Eagle® Brand Sweetened Condensed Milk (NOT evaporated)
½ cup ReaLime® Reconstituted Lime Juice
Few drops green food coloring, optional
½ teaspoon cream of tartar
⅓ cup sugar
Mint leaves, optional

Preheat oven to 350°. In medium bowl, beat egg yolks; stir in sweetened condensed milk, ReaLime and food coloring. In small bowl, stiffly beat 1 egg white; fold into sweetened condensed milk mixture. Turn into shell. Beat remaining egg whites with cream of tartar until foamy; gradually add sugar, beating until stiff but not dry. Spread meringue on top of pie; seal carefully to edge of shell. Bake 12 to 15 minutes or until meringue is golden brown. Cool. Chill before serving. If desired, garnish with mint leaves. Refrigerate leftovers.

*Use only Grade A clean, uncracked eggs.

TRADITIONAL PUMPKIN PIE
(Makes one 9-inch pie)

1 (9-inch) unbaked pastry shell
1 (16-ounce) can pumpkin (about 2 cups)
1 (14-ounce) can Eagle® Brand Sweetened Condensed Milk (NOT evaporated)
2 eggs
1 teaspoon ground cinnamon
½ teaspoon salt
½ teaspoon ground ginger
½ teaspoon ground nutmeg
Whipped cream and nuts, optional

Preheat oven to 425°. In large bowl, combine filling ingredients; mix well and turn into shell. Bake 15 minutes; reduce oven temperature to 350° and continue baking 35 to 40 minutes or until knife inserted 1 inch from edge comes out clean. Cool before cutting. If desired, garnish with whipped cream and nuts. Refrigerate leftovers.

These scrumptious and easy pie recipes might make you try a new homemade pie every week.

CHAPTER 5
Family Projects

Getting family members involved in family research can be a rewarding experience for all. Trying to find different ways to spark that interest can sometimes be a challenge in itself. Sharing family history information in a variety of ways with family members may be just the inspiration they need to begin their own ancestral quest. It can also foster new and stronger bonds among family researchers.

FAMILY REUNIONS

When we think of summertime, many of us think of family reunions. Family history always seems to be a big part of my family reunion. We share photographs, documents and stories. The family charts are updated throughout the year, and the most current one is displayed for everyone to enjoy.

If you are going to take family history information with you, you may want to make copies to share with others. I take my laptop, scanner, and personal color copier with me, but not everyone has these available or has electricity nearby. If you don't want your one-of-a-kind originals to get damaged or lost, you may want to make copies ahead of time to share with family members.

If you use genealogy software to keep track of your family files, make copies of the GEDCOM files and place them on diskette. A GEDCOM (Genealogical Data Communications) file is a standard file format for transferring genealogy files from one computer program to another. Remember to exclude personal information about living relatives before sharing your files. Most genealogy software has this feature built in to privatize data about living relatives. If not, use a program like GedCLEAN from RaynOrShyn Enterprises to prevent personal information from being given out when swapping family history information with others.

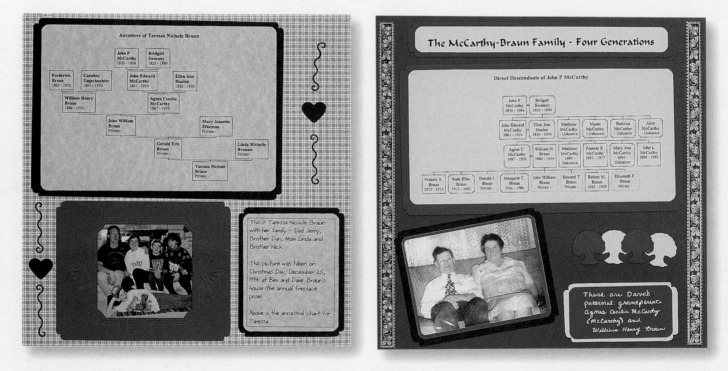

When you are sharing genealogy data with others, remember to use a feature to privatize data about living relatives as shown on the ancestral chart.

FAMILY REUNION SCRAPBOOK

If you hold annual family reunions, invite a few members of the extended family together to create a reunion scrapbook for past family reunions. Each member can work on a different year if you have enough information; or, have several people work on the same-year reunion collection. Include items such as photographs, guest list, and a copy of the invitation on your layout pages. Ask family members to write up a short highlights story which can include who traveled the farthest, who were the oldest and youngest family members at the reunion, and important details such as the date and place it was held, and who were the organizers. If family members brought potluck dishes or desserts, include some of the recipes and photos if you have them.

For your next family reunion, ask family members to create a layout page on loose cardstock of either 8½" x 11" or 12" x 12" from the previous reunion to bring with them. These can be placed in sheet protectors and hung on a large board during the reunion festivities. Afterward, place them in an archival album to be shared at future reunions with everyone.

Creating new pages from your annual family reunion is one way of celebrating your heritage with the rest of your family and it can be shared with future generations too.

Annual Kirschner Family Reunion – July 25, 1999 – held in Amelia, Ohio

The Steve Kirschner Family (above left): Tim + Linda Wollard, Mickey Stutz, Hubert + Wilma Stutz, (front row) Clinton + Kyle Wollard, Steve, Leigh Ann + Erika Stutz.
The Roy + Garnet Ernest Kirschner Family (above right): (backrow) Julie + Brittany, Troy + Debbie, Bill Oldiges (front row) Nancy with grandson Tyler, Ronnie, Garnet, Roy, Betty
Bottom Right: Richard Baker, Tiffany, Pat, Stephanie + Debbie Wahl Wetherell
Bottom Left: Family Heritage Cake made by my cousin Linda Kirschner Wollard

Kirschner Reunion – July, 1999
Above: Roy + Garnet, Maxine, Steve Kirschner

Above right in front: Cris, Derek, Erica, Barry Jr.
2nd Row: Josh, Lori, Mom (Maxine), Carol with Kelsey, Barry
3rd Row: Kelly, Alice
Last Row: Bev + Dave Braun, Steve holding Cody, Missy, Dan

Below: Eileen with daughters Donna, Lynn and Marilyn
First time they have all been together in 26 years

FAMILY NEWSLETTERS

Family newsletters can be a great source of information on everyday events in the lives of you and your family members. To make them interesting to others, you won't want to make the articles too short or include too much detail. Try to include a variety of stories that will have a broad appeal if you are going to distribute this to a fairly large number of family members.

Remember that if you have a large, extended family, not everyone will know one another. You may need to make brief references in your stories about what lineage the person has so others will know how they are related to one another. This will also help future generations understand relationships if these newsletters are kept with the rest of the family history information.

If this is the first newsletter you are attempting to write, most desktop publishing and word processing software include templates for newsletters. You can just edit these templates and include the information about your family.

As you become more comfortable at writing the newsletter, you can become more creative. For some great ideas for family newsletters, check out *Creating Family Newsletters* by Elaine Floyd, published by Betterway Books.

Family newsletters are a great way to help document and share your family history throughout the years. These books include tips to help you create a simple, interesting newsletter that your family members will want to read.

Tips for Better Newsletters

• In an opening paragraph, make a point to mention that the stories included in this newsletter may end up as part of your family heritage in the future. Some recipients may not see the value in the information you include in the newsletter. However, those of us who spend most of our spare time searching for family history news and information will treasure each of the newsletters. Most people don't write letters or send cards to family and friends anymore. If they write at all, they use e-mail. Everyday events will be harder to capture unless the electronic messages are printed and become part of your family history collection.

• Make the print large enough so that the readers don't have to strain to read the text. It should be between 12 and 14-point. Headlines should be larger (16-18 point) and in bold letters

• Don't include details of everything that has happened during the past year. Be selective and balance the good and the bad. Include a section where you can share family accomplishments giving the basic who, what, when, where, why and how.

• Include information on births, anniversaries and birthdays (include the month and day for the birthday and omit the year). After a certain age, not everyone may want the year of his or her birth published.

• Briefly discuss the unexpected crises, disappointing news such as major illnesses or accidents, deaths, or maybe a catastrophic event if a family member was a victim of a fire, flood, hurricane, or earthquake. It is best to check with the family involved first to be sure it is OK to share this information in the newsletter. If they agree, give just enough information to let family members know who was involved and what the general circumstances were. If readers want more information, they can personally contact the person or family involved. Too much detail may offend or cause a misunderstanding between family members if the information is not relayed and received in the right way.

• Include your e-mail address in the newsletter, and ask family members to submit information and stories to you to use in future newsletters. Ask if family members would like to receive the newsletter electronically rather than by regular snail mail. If they would, get their e-mail addresses from them. Sending the newsletter electronically is less expensive than having copies made and mailing them. It is also much quicker to distribute. Be sure to save it in a format that everyone will be able to access. Not everyone will have the most current versions of the same software you have.

• If you can get others to contribute information for the newsletter, try to include their information, editing what they submit if you need to. Family members will be more likely to contribute information in the future if they know you will share their stories in the newsletters.

• If you decide to include photographs, make sure you identify who is in the photograph and what the photograph is about.

FAMILY HISTORY WORD PUZZLES

There are several inexpensive types of software to create word games from your family history information. There are different levels of difficulty so you can make them easier for younger children and more difficult for the adults. You simply select the type of word puzzle you want to create, key in your clues and answers, and the software creates the puzzle (and the completed puzzle showing all the answers). These puzzles are not only fun to create but also a challenge to those filling them in to see if they can come up with the right answers.

You will be helping family members learn more about the details of their family history and, hopefully, getting them interested in doing some family history research themselves. It doesn't take much to get hooked on genealogy as a hobby. It is definitely one of the fastest growing hobbies in the world. Who knows, if more family members get involved in researching your ancestors, you might have enough help to put together several heritage albums from your family history information.

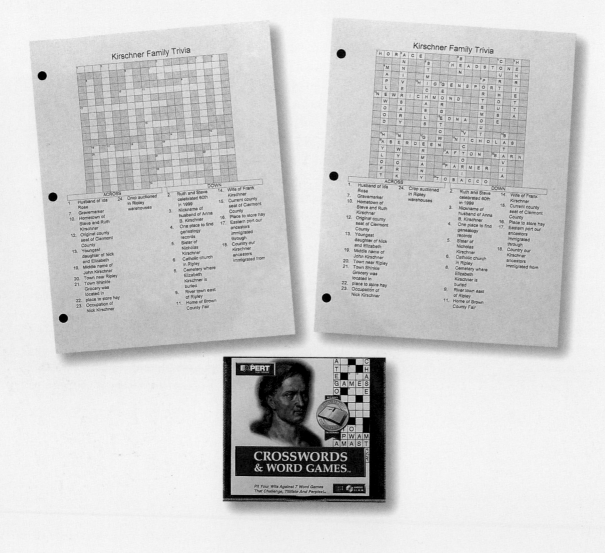

FAMILY TREE BOOKS FOR KIDS

MAKE YOUR OWN

To get the younger children interested in their family history, help them put together their own family history book. There are many styles of pre-printed acid-free scrapbook paper pages available in 8½" x 11" and 12" x 12" pages for just this purpose. You need to add family photographs and write in the family history information. Some adults I talked to have no idea who their grandparents and great-grandparents are. Don't let this happen in your family. Start your children and grandchildren early in their lives knowing their family history. It will help build their self-esteem and give them a sense of belonging by learning their heritage at an early age.

Spending time with a child putting together a family album will be a great time for both of you. Use a sturdy binder, and add sheet protectors on the pages. Children will want to share this with family and friends, and you won't want to worry about the pages getting dirty or torn. You can personalize the pages by adding some stickers and die-cuts to the pre-printed pages to make them special for your family history.

PURCHASED FAMILY BOOKS

Several books are available at the bookstores to create a family tree book for kids. These already include pre-printed pages for you to add photographs and genealogical details. These are a quick way to get a family history album completed for children and introduce them to their family ancestors.

These colorful preprinted papers make creating a family tree book with your kids fast and fun.

A variety of blank family tree books are available—just add photos and journaling to create your family history pages.

CHAPTER 6
Genealogy Online

Using the Internet offers so many opportunities for discovering your ancestors that it may be difficult to know where to begin. Some major misconceptions are that the Internet is the answer to everybody's questions. You will not be able to just type in a family name and have a completed family history pop up on your computer screen. You may, however, be able to speed up your research time and save on expenses along the way. Good old fashioned off-line research skills are still required to compliment today's technology.

WHERE DO I BEGIN?

If you are new to genealogy research, one of your first question might be, "Where do I begin?" One of the first things you will need to do before ever getting online is write down everything you know about your family history. Begin with yourself and work backward. There are two basic forms that you can use to get started documenting your family history—the ancestral and the pedigree charts. The information on these forms should include all of the names, dates and places you know about. Complete a chart for each line of the family tree you want to research. Do the same if you are researching family lines for your spouse or another person not related to you.

I covered general offline genealogical research techniques in my first book, *Crafting Your Own Heritage Album*. Included in the back of that book are some forms for you to copy and use for your research process. I also included general information on using genealogical software to help you organize and track your family history information on your computer. You will still need to utilize all of the

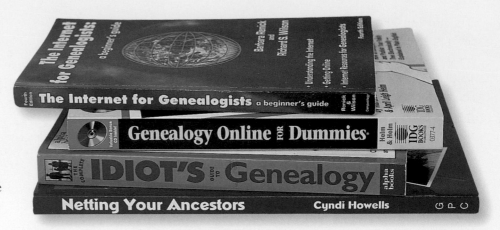

Books and magazines can be of great assistance. Genealogy-specific magazines can offer lots of useful information for both online and offline research by covering topics on the newest and the latest in research tools and techniques, and the best web sites for what you are looking for.

other traditional offline research methodologies for your genealogical research. Going online and using the Internet is just one more very powerful research option now available to you whenever you have time to sit down at the computer and take advantage of the information that is available to you.

Keep in mind that you will not be able to type a surname into a database and come out with a completed family

history report. The Internet is going to be another source that you can add to the list of tools already available to you, such as libraries, the LDS Family History Centers, printed family histories, genealogical societies, professional organizations and researchers, etc., but it is not the only tool you need or should use. With the Internet you now have an online tool that is available twenty-four hours a day, seven days a week. If you need a dictionary, a map, forms, an address on where to send for something, or if you want to trade information with someone on the other side of the globe, the Internet will be available whatever time of the day you are working.

Primary and Secondary Sources

The primary purpose of any genealogical research is to systematically search for specific information and then validate it ultimately with primary source documents. The Internet will not contain digital copies of all the documents available throughout the world for each ancestor you may want to research—the same way no one book or one facility contains all of the copies you may be looking for. It can, however, significantly speed up the time it takes to locate these sources and save you money by doing so.

One thing you must keep in mind is that even though you find printed information on the Internet, this does not mean it is true and/or accurate. All of the records were originally compiled by humans and are prone to mistakes. Don't just trust the information you find unless you have some official source of information to validate it, which is where your primary and secondary source documents come in.

Primary sources are records of events from an eyewitness at the time of the event or shortly thereafter, documents that were recorded by someone who had direct knowledge of the event, such as a baptismal record completed by the attending church official. Other primary source documents would include letters, diaries, family Bibles that have birth, marriage and death dates associated with the names, video or voice recordings, oral family history accounts, census records and firsthand newspaper accounts.

Copies of primary and second documents will validate the information you collect on your ancestral heritage.

Secondary sources are seen as those documents or information where the information may have come from a secondhand source. A death certificate can have both primary and secondary information on it. Information about the date and circumstances of the death may be completed by a physician or a coroner at the time of the death and are considered primary sources. However, a family member or friend who may not know the accurate details may provide some information pertaining to specific information about the individual.

VITAL RECORDS

Vital records were created because an event had enough significance or was importance enough that it was documented and the record was collected and maintained by some level of the government. This includes documents such as birth, marriage, death, naturalization, and passports.

Do Your Homework

If you are new to using a computer and are not yet familiar with the Internet, I recommend you refer to some of the books in the resource guide in the back of this book. Go to the library or local bookstore, read through some of these books, and select one to learn more about going online. If you don't already have a personal computer, most public libraries have computers connected to the Internet. You can spend a little time using their computers before you invest a lot of time and money in a computer system at home, just to be sure this is something you are going to feel comfortable with.

There are numerous articles, journals, and entire specialty books on all aspects of researching online using the Internet, from the basics to very technical how-to manuals. Here are just a few of the things you'll need to know about:

- computer hardware and a modem
- software for your PC's operating system
- Internet software

There is also an enormous amount of information about what you can find once you get online. You'll need to know some of the basic terminology and where to look in order to make your time online useful and efficient. A few of the basics include how to determine an objective and develop a search plan, what types of search tools are available for genealogists and what types of information they will help you find once you get online, how you should begin your search (depending on your search objective), and what kind of genealogy software you need to organize the information you collect.

I want to try to explain some of the very basic terms and information you will need to know. I can't begin to give you enough detailed information to adequately prepare you for researching online. There are resources in the back for books, magazines and web sites that will steer you in the right direction. You will have to read through some of these to prepare yourself for your online adventures. Your experience online will not be productive if you don't read and educate yourself. You will get discouraged and possibly give up. Don't. There is so much valuable information on the Internet for you to discover and make part of your family history. You just need to figure out the best way to find the information that is of most value to your research and take advantage of it.

NEW IDEAS FOR CRAFTING HERITAGE ALBUMS

GENEALOGY SOFTWARE

Genealogy software offers a wide variety of features—some you will want to use, some not. Do some research to see how the products differ and select one based on what you want to do with the information you collect. Most genealogy magazines and journals offer current reviews of many of the popular programs and their features.

Some of the primary reasons you will want to consider using genealogical software to aid in your family history research include the following:

• It will help you organize your family history information.

• It will help you sort and search for data quickly and easily. You'll be able to find individuals and information about them by entering specific data such as name and dates.

• You will be able to create charts and reports to see exactly where new entries into your file fit into the overall family tree.

• You can keep track of all those little bits of information that you don't know what to do with.

• Most will allow you to create a research journal that you can print and work from the next time you are doing online or offline research so you can pick up where you left off.

• Many will let you add pictures, sound, documents, etc., to create a digital family history file.

• You can avoid adding duplicates and check for errors on individuals you already have (like when a child's birth date is after the death of a parent).

Versions of these software packages change frequently, and new enhancements and features are included. Many of the Internet web sites for genealogy software offer demo copies so you can try before you buy. This is a good idea. Sometimes just the way the data is presented to you on the computer screen may not be pleasing to you. Select a software package that has the most agreeable features to what your goals are for your family history research. Try different views, print sample reports, and try creating a custom report to see if you get the results you expect. Ask family and friends what software they use and what they like most about it.

Note: When you are entering dates on your forms, on research sheets, or into your genealogical software, the formats need to be consistent. Dates should always be written as day-month-year using the three-letter abbreviation for the month: 03 Aug 1856. When you look at this date, there is no doubt that it means the third of August 1856. If the date is written as 08/03/56 or even 08/03/1856, it can be misunderstood by someone else who is reading it. It may be difficult to tell if the month is August or March and what century you are referring to. Always use the full year in all of your documentation. Your research can span ancestors over several centuries, and many of them will have the same names. The only differentiation in many cases is the dates associated with that specific ancestor.

ONLINE KNOW-HOW

As I said before, there is a lot of information about the Internet that you will need to know to make your online time productive. Here is a brief description of some terms and useful information that will get you started. To learn more about the specifics of the information, refer to the resources in the back of this book. There is also a vast amount of information available at the library and local bookstores about researching on the Internet.

TOOLS TO USE

There are many tools and techniques available to use to pursue ancestral data online. There is no single online tool or technique that will be the answer to all of your investigative searches. No one tool can be used successfully in all cases. By gaining an understanding of each of these online tools, you will be much more successful. You will also be able to work around some of the weaknesses of these online tools if you take the time to become more familiar with how they actually work.

There are several tools you can use to help you take advantage of the information that is available on the Net. Some of these tools include:

- World Wide Web (WWW or sometimes just the Web)
- mailing lists
- file transfer protocol (FTP)
- telnet
- electronic mail or e-mail

None of these tools provides the best access to online genealogy data by itself. You will need to take the time to learn about each one of these a little more to see if it is a tool that can help in your quest for family history data.

WORLD WIDE WEB

There is a lot of technical detail about how the World Wide Web actually works, and I'm not going to go into too much detail here. Your eyes will probably just glaze over and you won't want to read it anyway. If you are interested in more detailed information, there are a lot of sources available.

Just to give you a general overview, the Web starts out with powerful host computers, called servers, that hold the data that makes up the Web pages you view, the actual documents. The files are named and are linked together so the server knows which files to pull up when you click on a link. These links are based on URLs, or Uniform Resource Locator, that tell the service which file you want. When you click on the link, your Web browser tells the server to get the printed text and graphics that go together. They are loaded on the screen and display much like a printed text page would.

For those of you who use America Online (AOL), keep in mind that AOL is not the Internet. It is a huge collection of proprietary information that has been collected for databases to assist members in easily finding whatever information they need. But it is not the true Internet. If you use only the information found on AOL, you are limiting yourself to only one source of information available to you on the World Wide Web.

MAILING LISTS

There are many Internet-based special interest groups, also known as mailing lists or discussion groups, that are dedicated to genealogy. There are thousands of genealogy mailing lists.

Web Site Address Endings

.com — indicates the site is a commercial site, which includes corporate home pages or individual home pages. Commercial sites provide reliable information about product information, business enterprises, online technical support for hardware and software, and many provide online ordering capabilities for products.

.gov — indicates the site is an official government entity, usually the federal government. These sites can be deemed reliable as they are responsible for providing their constituents with accurate information on regulations, finances, laws, etc.

.edu — indicates an educational institution such as a college, university, or other school computer system operates this site. Examine the information carefully as these sites contain both authentic and superficial information, depending on the school's policy for its users.

.mil — indicates a military organization, such as the Pentagon.

.net — indicates a networking company, such as an ISP, operates the site.

.org — indicates nonprofit organization or associations run the site. If researching a specific area, you can obtain a great deal of credible information from professional and research organizations.

Many of these are centered on geographic interests (those with ancestors in Ireland or Indiana), military interests (Civil War or WWII), or ethnic groups (Jewish or African American). Mailing lists make it easy to find other researchers who are interested in the same topics, surnames and locales you are researching.

Subscribing to or joining one of these groups is much like joining a club or organization except you don't have to pay any fees or dues to join. To join you just send an e-mail message to the computer that distributes the messages to all of the users on the mailing list for that group. There is usually a specific way to subscribe (join) and unsubscribe (discontinue) your participation in a mailing list group. Be sure to read and follow the instructions exactly and keep a copy for future reference.

Most experienced researchers suggest you use a different e-mail address for posting messages than you do for subscribing to lists. After you join a new group, don't jump right in and start sending out long messages or queries to the group. Read the incoming messages from the group for about a week or more to get to know how the group works and the type of information they send and receive. Find out how the group responds to messages. Some people respond to the group as a whole, and some will respond directly to you.

FILE TRANSFER PROTOCOL (FTP)

FTP is an application that allows users to send and receive files between remote computers. It allows you to upload and download computer files from one computer to another. When

you download a file from the Web, your computer normally retrieves it using FTP. FTP is also used to upload files so that they can be viewed on the World Wide Web. If you are transferring a large file to someone, it is almost always best to use FTP rather than e-mail. FTP is much better suited for this than e-mail. You can download a file to a disk, disconnect from the remote computer, and then view or execute the file on the local machine without having to stay connected over a telephone line to the remote computer.

You may also hear the term anonymous FTP. This allows a user to receive files from a remote computer without having to have an account on the remote system. Some commercial sites maintain anonymous FTP sites for the convenience of their customers so they can download updates for program files to their machines without having to request diskettes through the mail.

TELNET

Telnet is an application that allows you, as a user, to connect to a remote computer and use it as if your own computer were connected directly to that computer. It will allow the user to run programs that are based on that remote machine. Telnet sites can access such things as databases and library catalogs.

E-MAIL

There are specific guidelines for using e-mail and dos and don'ts that you need to know before you start sending messages. Otherwise, you can easily offend someone on the receiving end of the message and she will not want

to help you with your research.

First, be clear when writing messages. This is essential for online communication. You must include all of the relevant information pertaining to your request, including important names, dates, and places pertaining to the question being asked. Keep the information short and concise, but don't leave out important details. People reading this message on the other end need to have a general idea of just how much research effort and time you've spent already. You can give information about the parents or siblings of the individual that you are researching to help others make a better connection.

E-MAIL ETIQUETTE

Before sending a detailed, lengthy e-mail message to someone you have not corresponded with before, send a short introductory message first. Tell the person in a brief paragraph or two about your interest in genealogy. Don't go into a lot of detail until you find out if they share your interest in family history. Some Internet users may have to pay for each e-mail message they send and receive, so don't waste their time or their money without knowing if they want to hear from you. Otherwise, you may have cost yourself a friend and a potential research partner.

E-mail is not private and never assume it is. Even if it has been deleted, it can still be recovered and read if necessary. Don't send personal or confidential information to a group forum, even if it is available somewhere else on the Internet. You can never be sure how and where that information may be used in the future.

RESEARCH ONLINE

The first thing you should understand is that all of the extensive holdings of available genealogical data throughout the world is not available online. There are thousands of books, rolls of microfiche and microfilm, and documents in the United States alone that are not yet available on the Internet.

Even if you find family history information online, it must be validated. You will need to reference the original documents in the library, local courthouses, and public libraries to verify the information you find as accurate and complete. The indexes online may give only a very limited amount of the information the original document contains.

To help you prepare for what type of information you can search for online, refer to books and magazine, listed in the resource sections. These will help you determine if it is worth your while to search online for these records or whether the records may be available only in a certain research facility. If you are an experienced researcher, I hope some of these sites will give you additional information to help you achieve success during your online research. These sites will provide you with

- information on basic research techniques
- tips on how to avoid common pitfalls that will leave you frustrated and confused
- tips on successful research strategies
- forms you can download for free to help you write down what you already know
- search databases for document indexes to find a match on family surnames
- portal sites to mailing lists,

There are numerous reference books that will help you make the most of both with your online and offline family history search.

bulletin boards, chat rooms and message boards to find people searching in the same locale or searching the same surnames you are

USING A SEARCH PLAN

There is just too much genealogical information on the World Wide Web for you to read through all the Web sites. One key to finding the information you want among all of the databases and Web sites is to begin by creating an established search plan. This will help you stay focused and on track with your research. It will also help you keep track of some of the most useful Web sites you have searched and eliminate others.

Without a search plan, you will be wandering around the Internet just like you would if you went to a super mall looking for a gift without any idea what you were looking for. Before going online, decide what you want to find. Here are a few suggestions to help you

get started creating a search plan. What are you looking for?

- census records for a specific period of time and locale
- land records
- birth records
- a marriage certificate
- someone else who is researching the same ancestral lines you are

Without a good search plan, you can easily become frustrated with all of the information available and how little information you find that is useful to your research. This can also lead to false assumptions when your searches do not turn up ancestors you are searching for. You assume that they are not there and may go on to something else. In fact, they may be in the database you are searching, but you are unable to find them because you may not be using good search techniques. If you get stuck while searching online, try checking out the research bulletin boards to see what successes others have had and what techniques they use to find their ancestors.

Internet Research Log

Ancestor's Name:	Gouge – Grant County, Ky – California Connection		
What are you looking for? Gouge / Williams		**URL Address Searched:** www.usgennet.org	
DATE	**Type of Record Searched**	**Information found that may be relevant to search?**	**What follow-up is required to validate information found**
11/15/00	Family Histories	Gonge, Eliza	name could be Gouge
11/15	Marriages-Grant County, Ky	1820 –1828 None found	N/A
11/15	http://gouge~1@rootsweb.com CA Death INDEX	Marietta Gouge	Marietta rather than Henrietta – name + dates in Ky + CA Are the same
			OBTain Death Certificate from CA – printed forms
Prepared by:			
Date:			

c:\data\genforms\internetresearch

Using a research form can help you keep track of what information you find online and where and when. It will also help you eliminate sites that are not useful to your search right now.

Internet Research Log

Ancestor's Name:			
What are you looking for?		**URL Address Searched:**	
DATE	**Type of Record Searched**	**Information found that may be relevant to search?**	**What follow-up is required to validate information found**
Prepared by:			
Date:			

c:\data\genforms\internetresearch

SEARCH ENGINES

There are several large web sites that specialize in providing free search engines to web pages. A search engine is a utility that locates resources via searches for keywords and phrases that you type in a search box. Each search engine is designed a little differently from the others. They will not return the same results even if you type in the same search words. Standard search engines do not find every single web page on the Internet.

Most screens include a search box on them. If you begin your online search by typing in the word *genealogy*, you will soon find out that there are several thousand sites that include a reference to genealogy. A better way to begin your search is to combine at least two words, such as *Irish Genealogy* or *Bristol Family* to narrow your search choices .

When you begin to use the search engines, spend the time reading their help section on each site. Each search engine handles the search words differently, and depending upon how it handles those words, each site will return different results. If you use more than one word in your search string, the search engine may default to *and*, or it may default to *or*. The help section will tell you what the defaults are so you know exactly how to enter your search string to get the results you want. It will save you time and help you find what you are looking for that much faster.

Some sites use Boolean logic, which means they allow you to use words rather than characters to filter your search. These are terms like *and*, *or*, *near*, and *and not*. Again, these are explained on each Web search engine page. You'll need to find out exactly how to use them so you get the results you want.

STANDARD SEARCH ENGINES

Just a few of the standard search engines are

- Excite
  http://www.excite.com
- Infoseek
  http://www.infoseek.com
- Google
  http://www.google.com
- Northern Light
  http://www.northernlight.com
- AltaVista
  http://www.altavista.com
- WebCrawler
  http://www.webcrawler.com

GENEALOGY SEARCH ENGINES

You will want to use multiple search engines during your online research. If you can't find the information you are looking for, try another search engine. There are several search engines that are specific to genealogy research and will be more useful than others. However, no single search engine will return everything that is available on the Internet.

Genealogy search engines scour specific databases or genealogy-only sites rather than searching all sites on the Internet. There are genealogy-specific sites that search for particular types of genealogy information. There are thousands of genealogy-specific web sites that can assist you in your research. Many of those are listed in the genealogy resources at the back of the book, including these two examples:

- Bureau of Land Management
  www.blm.gov
- Census Records
  www.census.com

Common Search Engine Commands

- Putting one or more words between quotation marks tells the search engine to look for those words in a phrase. Use quotation marks around proper name such as "Manchester, England" so it finds Web pages with that phrase in it instead of thousands with just the word *England* or *Manchester*.

- An asterisk is used as a wildcard. If you enter a term such as *photo*, it will find sites with the words *photo*, *photograph*, *photography*, *photographer*, *photographs*.

- Putting a plus sign in front of a word means the sites must contain all of the words in the string, such as *Genealogy + Baltimore + Maryland*.

- Putting a minus sign means the web page should not contain that word or words.

Outdated Medical Terms

When you are searching old records, especially hospital records and death certificates, you will come across some old medical terms that you may not be familiar with. At right is a list of a few of those terms. There are reference books in the library and web sites online where you can reference more information on medical terms if you come across one that is not listed here.

Outdated Term	New Term
acute mania	severe insanity
ague	used to define the recurring fever and chills of malarial infection
apoplexy	stroke
bad blood	syphilis
Bright's disease	glomerulonephritis (serious kidney disease)
camp fever	typhus
chorea (St. Vitus' dance)	nervous disorder
consumption	tuberculosis
cretinism	hypothyroidism, congenital
dropsy	congestive heart failure
falling sickness	epilepsy
fatty liver	cirrhosis
glandular fever	mononucleosis
jail fever	typhus
lockjaw	tetanus
lung fever	pneumonia
lung sickness	tuberculosis
mania	insanity
nostalgia	homesickness
putrid fever	diphtheria
quinsy	tonsillitis
remitting fever	malaria
screws	rheumatism
septicemia	blood poisoning
ship's fever	typhus

FAMILY RELATIONSHIP TERMS

When you are working on your family history, sometimes it is helpful to know how to describe family relationships more precisely. Here are some definitions that should help you, whether you are the one using them or you come across them in your research.

• Cousin (first cousin)—your first cousins are the children of your aunts and uncles. They are members of your family who have two of the same grandparents as you do.

• Second cousin—these are family members who have the same great-grandparents as you do but not the same grandparents.

• Third, fourth and fifth cousins—third cousins have the same g-g-grandparents; fourth cousin family members have the same g-g-g-grandparents; fifth cousins have the same g-g-g-g-grandparents and so on.

• Removed—when this term is used, it means that the two people being described in the relationship are from different generations. The term once removed means there is one generation difference between you; twice removed means there is a two-generation difference.

Below is a relationship table that should help you figure out the exact relationship of different family members and terminology to use when describing family members.

1. Select any two people in your family and determine what ancestor they have in common. An example: If you select yourself and one of your cousins, you both would have the same common grandparent.

2. Next look at the top row and find the first person's relationship to that common ancestor. Your cousin would be the grandchild of your grandparent.

3. Then look at the first column on the left and find the second person's relationship to that same common ancestor. You would also be the grandchild of your grandparent.

4. Go across the chart and find the correct row and column that shows where those two relationships meet. The intersecting row and column would be "first cousin" for the two of you since your common ancestor would be a grandparent.

Common Ancestor	Child	Grandchild	Great Grandchild	Great-Great Grandchild
Child	brother or sister	nephew or niece	grandnephew or grandniece	great-grandnephew or great-grandniece
Grandchild	Nephew or Niece	first cousin	first cousin, once removed	first cousin, twice removed
Great-Grandchild	grandnephew or grandniece	first cousin, once removed	second cousin	second cousin, once removed
Great-Great-Grandchild	great-grandnephew or great-grandniece	first cousin, once removed	second cousin, once removed	third cousin

AMERICAN SOUNDEX TABLE

A Soundex is not an alphabetic index; it is a phonetic index. The key feature to Soundex is that it codes surnames (last names) based on the way a name sounds rather than on how it is spelled.

Soundexing was first used for the 1880 census in 1935. It was created as a means of providing birth information for the newly created Social Security System. It was not designed for the genealogical researcher. The Rand Corporation was hired by the Census Bureau to formulate a phonetic coding system. Hundreds of Works Progress Administration (WPA) workers created the Soundex indexes. Most last names can be spelled in a variety of ways, for example "Smith" can also be spelled "Smythe," "Smithe," and "Smyth."

The WPA workers created Soundex cards for the heads of households for the 1880, 1900 and 1920 censuses. The cards were then arranged in order by the Soundex codes. The Soundex system has become a great tool for genealogists by identifying spelling variations for a given surname.

When searching online, check to see if the Soundex index feature is available. In many cases it is not, especially when you are searching indices that are just scanned or transcribed copies of the original records. However, if it is available take advantage of it. It can certainly help you find leads on surnames that you may not have considered before.

To use the Soundex index feature, you must first create the code for your surname. On this page is the table used to convert surnames from alphabetic to the phonetic Soundex system. Each Soundex code consists of one letter and three numbers, such as R216, no matter how long the name is. The letter is always the first letter of the surname (S for Smith). The rest of the consonants in the name determine the numbers in the code, and the vowels are always ignored.

There is a lot more information about the Soundex system available online and at the library if you want more details about how to use it more effectively.

Soundex Table

1	b, f, p, v
2	c, g, j, k, g, s, x, z
3	d, t
4	l
5	m, n
6	r
no code	a, e, h, i, o, u, y, w

GALLERY

Triangle corner borders and paper doilies showcase these heritage photographs.

Ida (top left) and Belle McCormick (top right)
Mother McCormick of Grand Rapids, Michigan – 1910

Dress up old-time photographs with pretty paper and fancy pre-cut frames.

Ben and Mamie Sosby Rheinschmidt
Grandma Lizzie's brother & sister-in-law

The photo on the left is of Ben Rheinschmidt at his wake. His coffin is on the front porch of his house. It was common practice up through the first quarter of the 19th Century to take pictures at funerals and of family and friends on their deathbed. This was the only picture we had of Uncle Ben for quite a few years, until family members brought these other photos to our Family Reunion to share.

A Puzzle Mate template was used to create one page (left) of a two-page layout. To complement the template layout, journaling and some of the original sunflower seeds from the garden were added to the second page (below).

Summer Vegetable Garden Provides Year Round Food

Our vegetable garden was one of the most important parts of our daily lives from spring until late fall every year. My father grew almost every vegetable that we ate year-round. Fresh vegetables from spring until fall and canned vegetables through the winter months. We had several varieties of tomatoes, carrots, bell peppers, cabbage, corn, turnips, potatoes, green beans, peas, lettuce, onions and more. Canning season was a huge process each autumn at our house. Everyone pitched in and spent days getting the fresh vegetables canned so we would have plenty of food for the winter. Dad always had so many vegetables that there were plenty for the neighbors too.

One year Dad decided to plant some giant sunflower seeds just to see how tall they would get. In the bottom right picture, you can see they went wild that year. Some of them were 12-15ft tall. The birds had a feast that year. We saved many of the seeds and a few of them remain in the envelope below. We made our own bird feed using a piece of toast covered with peanut butter and sunflower seeds to put outside during the winter.

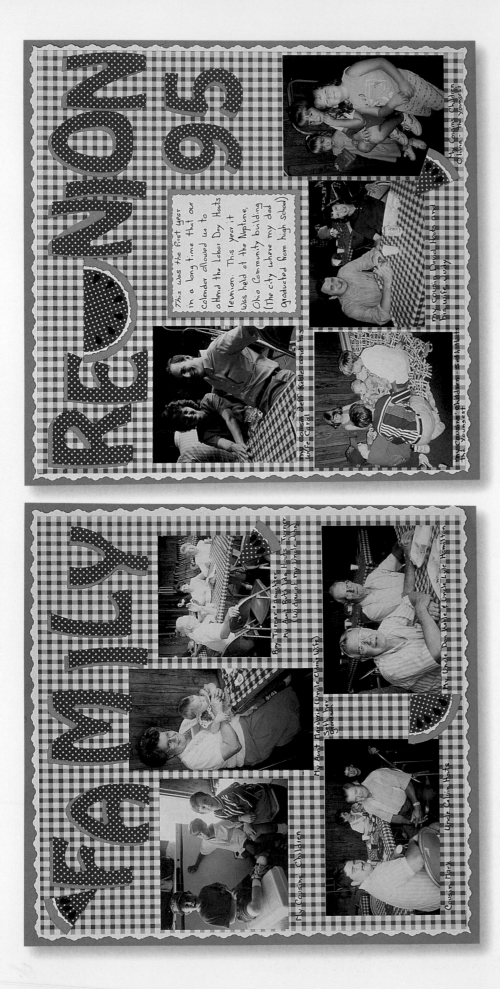

Family reunions hold special memories for everyone. This two-page layout highlights those memories with photos and journaling.

Acid-free paper hearts and pretty paper enhance the romance of this engagement design.

Use craft punches to add a three-dimensional embellishment.

FAMILY GATHERINGS

Top Left: Erica, Alice, Terry and Brian Davis - Christmas at Bev & Dave's
Top right: Bev & Dave Braun with Carrie Lynn Kirschner
Bottom Left: Carrie with her two Grandmothers on her 16th Birthday:
Jane Thielmeyer and Maxine Kirschner, February 4, 1999
Bottom Right: The Braun Brothers at Bill's 80th Birthday Party - Dec. 11, 1999 - Bill, Don & Ed

Add photos and journaling to a pre-cut frame, and paper-punched squares and alphabet stickers for classic-looking layouts.

Bring your black and white photos to life using some of the beautiful papers now available.

Family Gathering

Summertime Fun....

Almost every Sunday afternoon in the summer, Mom's family would come up to the farm for dinner and to visit. We lived about 25 miles east of Cincinnati, Ohio. The "city folks" always had such a good time. It would take about hour to drive from the West side of town where most of lived at the time - early 1960's.

Maxine, Sue, Grandma Marie, Bev

Alice Joy, Mother Marie, Barbara Anne, Ethel Nae, Maxine, Duane

Nae, Warren, Barb, Worth, Don, Ethel, Mother Marie + Father Warren "Dusty"

Paper-punched flowers create a lovely enhancement on this portrait.

Helen Lucille Long
1945

Mary Jeannette Efkeman Braun
with younger sister
Helen Virginia Efkeman Hammond.

Top: abt. 1931- Mary at age 10 & Ginny at age 6.

Bottom: abt. 1929 - Mary at age 8 & Ginny at age 4

Intricate acid-free lace photo frames are ideal for showing off your heritage photographs.

Photos of siblings taken decades apart show how little or how much family members change over the years.

These elegant photo frames make stunning layout pages.

NEW IDEAS FOR CRAFTING HERITAGE ALBUMS

Photographs of Bev's Maternal Grandparents - Warren John and Anna Marie Droll Millennor.
Top Left - May 22, 1954 - attending the wedding of their daughter, Ethel to Clarence Bader
Top Right - April 1948 - outside Burdett Avenue apartment in Walnut in Cincinnati, Ohio
Bottom Left: 42nd Wedding Anniversary - Sept 13, 1959 - at Ethel & Clarence Bader's house
Bottom Right: August 10, 1949 - John & Margie Stephen and Marie and Warren Millennor at
Coney Island in Cincinnati, Ohio

Include important details with your photographs to commemorate important events in your ancestor's lives.

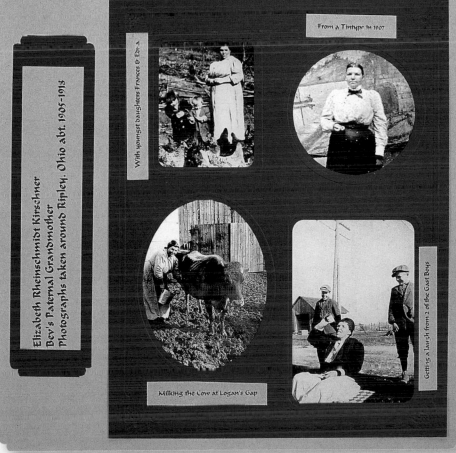

Elizabeth Rheinschmidt Kirschner
Bev's Paternal Grandmother
Photographs taken around Ripley, Ohio, abt. 1905-1918

From a Tintype in 1907

With youngst Daughters Frances & Elva

Milking the Cow at Logan's Gap

Getting a laugh from 2 of the Gast Boys

The photo in the top right corner of this frame was scanned and cleaned up from an old blackened tintype photograph.

Several photographs of one ancestor can be displayed in a collage frame to show a glimpse of the changes over the years.

Nicholas Kirschner
Sept 1, 1869 - June 22, 1953
Bev's Paternal Grandfather

1952 - In front of Shinkle Grocery, Afton, Oh - Age 82

1895 - Wedding Photo Ripley, Ohio - Age 26

Left: Autumn 1916 - Scoffield Rd Farm Ripley, Ohio - age 47
Right: 1940 - Dixon Ridge Farm Ripley-Day Hill Rd Ripley, Ohio - age 71

Stella and Charles Anderson
25th Wedding Anniversary Portrait
Sacramento, California
June 15, 1968

A pre-embossed frame with an attractive embellishment offers a striking design to showcase photos.

Pictures of the youngest members of the family will become the heritage photographs of the future.

Photocopy magazines and newspaper articles to include on your heritage pages to capture the story behind the memories.

School photographs are an important part of our family history.

Balancing a layout with lots of photos is easy using the Plan-a-Page templates from EK Success.

NEW IDEAS FOR CRAFTING HERITAGE ALBUMS

Including photographs and information on a family business is an excellent way of documenting your heritage.

Photocopying memorabilia too large to include in your album captures the essence of significant events and achievements in our lives.

NEW IDEAS FOR CRAFTING HERITAGE ALBUMS

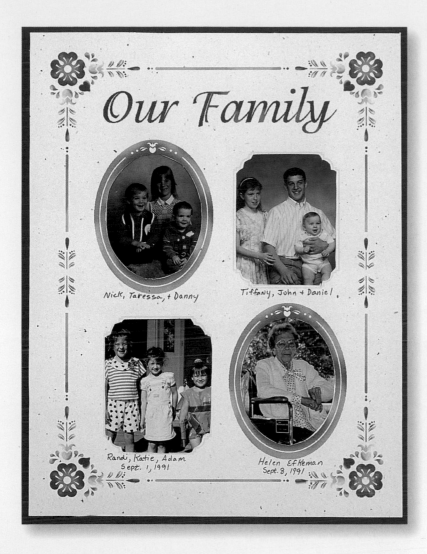

Computer generated layouts offer many choices for your heritage album.

Corner borders printed off a computer add a floral frame to this photo.

The Thomas Calvert Family Heritage Album
Three Generations

Calvert Family and In-Laws:
Back Left: Thomas, Mary Jane, Ella, Sadie Jobs, Clarence Calvert, Ernest Yager, Richard Calvert, John Jobs
Front: Truman Calvert, Libby Yager, Edna and Helen Jobs, Bonnie Calvert.

Title pages can help keep family history information organized.

Photos and information of ancestors' occupations is an important part of documenting your heritage.

Gold Miners in Cripple Creek, Colorado

The photograph above was taken outside one of the many Gold mines near Cripple Creak, Colorado on October 18, 1900. These miners were part of the gold rush days that hit this area and put Cripple Creak on the map in 1890. In 1899, $59 million in gold ore was taken out of the ground and sent out of the camp.

The photo on the right was taken a several years later around the Colorado Springs area.

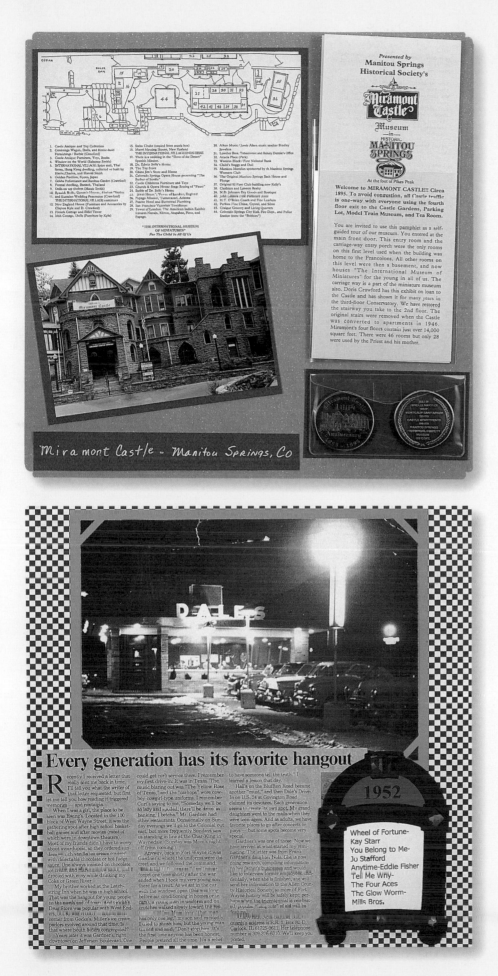

Miramont Castle - Manitou Springs, CO

Document historical homes and events that hold special memories for you.

Color photocopy newspaper articles about family businesses to include in your album for future generations to enjoy.

Scrapbook Resources

The Archival Company
P.O. Box 101
Holyoke, MA 01040
Phone: (800) 442-7576 (free catalog)
www.archivalcompany.com
Materials for the preservation of photos and collectibles, including museum-quality albums, scrapbooks, storage boxes, other holiday gift ideas

Avery Dennison Consumer Service Center
50 Pointe Dr.
Brea, CA 92821
Phone: (800) 462-8379
Fax: (800) 831-2496
www.avery.com
Archival binders, dividers, acid-free sheet protectors

Canson-Talens, Inc.
21 Industrial Ave.
South Hadley, MA 01075
(800) 628-9283
Acid-free paper, archival binders, artistic materials and supplies

Center for Life Stories Preservation
137 Bates Ave.
St. Paul, MN 55106-6328
www.storypreservation.com
Resource for capturing family and life stories and memoirs. Easy how-to books, plus a web site full of free tips and ideas (interviewing, memory triggering, publishing).

Century Craft
Phone: (800) 340-2031
Archival-quality page protectors

Chatterbox, Inc.
252 Main St.
P.O. Box 216
Star, ID 83669
Phone: (877) 722-4288
Fax: (208) 286-9828
www.chatterboxpub.com
E-mail: info@chatterboxpub.com
Innovative product line to simplify the process of journaling, plus templates and border tools and small books on journaling

Close to My Heart
1199 W. 700 S.
Pleasant Grove, UT 84062
Phone: (888) 655-6552
Fax: (801) 763-8188
www.dotadventures.com
Acid-free, lignin-free papers, scrapbook supplies, page protectors, rubber stamps and inks

Cock-A-Doodle Design, Inc.
3759 W. 2340 S., Suite D
Salt Lake City, UT 84120
Phone: (800) 262-9727
Acid-free, lignin-free page toppers, page doodler markers, page frames, page pieces, page pocket guides, page printables

Creative Card Company
1500 W. Monroe St.
Chicago, IL 60607
Phone: (312) 666-8686
E-mail: ccinquiry@aol.com
Embossed photo frames and mattes, archival paper

Creative Memories
3001 Clearwater Rd.
P.O. Box 1839
St. Cloud, MN 56302-1839
Phone: (800) 468-9335
www.creativememories.com
Direct sales through consultants offering photo-safe scrapbook albums and accessories

Creative Xpress!
295 W. Center St.
Provo, UT 84601
www.coluzzle.com
www.creativexpress.com
Phones: (800) 563-8679
(801) 373-6838 (24-hour)
Fax: (801) 373-1446
E-mail: sales@creativexpress.com
Award-winning Coluzzle Cutting System, which lets you create custom collage puzzles and photo page layouts from templates

Crop in Style
Platte Productions
20540 Superior St. #D
Chatsworth, CA 91311-4445

Phone: (888) 700-2202
Fax: (818) 700-9728
www.cropinstyle.com
E-mail: support @cropinstyle.com
Totes and binders for all your scrapbook supplies

The C-Thru Ruler Company
6 Britton Dr.
P.O. Box 356
Bloomfield, CT 06002
Phone: (860) 243-0303
Fax: (860) 243-1856
www.cthruruler.com
C-Thru rulers, stencils, templates, edgers, 3D Keepers, acid-free alphabet letters

Cut-It-Up
4543 Orange Grove Ave.
Sacramento, CA 95841
Phone: (916) 482-2288
Supply totes for all your scrapbooking supplies, Ruler-It-Up rulers and idea books, creative lettering idea books

EK Success Ltd.
125 Entin Rd.
Clifton, NJ 07014-1141
Phone: (800) 524-1349
Fax: (800) 767-2963
www.eksuccess.com
Zig Memory System and Photo Twin pens, paper shaper punches, memory pencils, Jell-Pop archival pens, adhesives, Border Buddy borders, corners and alphabet templates, Circle Scissor and Circle Ruler

Emagination Crafts
530 N. York Rd.
Bensenville, IL 60106
Phone: (630) 238-9770
www.emaginationcrafts.com
Unique collection of paper craft punches, photo-mounting corners and decorative scissors

Epson America, Inc.
3840 Kilroy Airport Way
Long Beach, CA 90806
Phone: (800) 533-3731
Fax: (562) 290-5536
www.epson.com